AN INDUCTIVE APPROACH TO BIBLICAL STUDY

Philip B. Harner

UNIVERSITY
PRESS OF
AMERICA

Copyright © 1982 by

University Press of America,™ Inc.

4720 Boston Way
Lanham, MD 20706

3 Henrietta Street
London WC2E 8LU England

Library of Congress Cataloging in Publication Data

Harner, Philip B.
  An inductive approach to biblical study.

  1. Bible–Text-books. I. Title.
BS605.2.H36   1982   220.6'1   82–40213
ISBN 0–8191–2608–X
ISBN 0–8191–2609–8 (pbk.)

All University Press of America books are produced on acid-free
paper which exceeds the minimum standards set by the National
Historical Publications and Records Commission.

TABLE OF CONTENTS

PART ONE: THE OLD TESTAMENT

PART TWO: THE NEW TESTAMENT

PREFACE

This study guide to the Bible consists of questions on major writings in the Old Testament and all the books of the New Testament. Most of the questions are designed to help a student become familiar with the content of biblical passages and the distinctive ideas or perspectives of biblical writers. Some questions introduce the student to the methods of biblical study and theories of authorship and composition. Still other questions ask the student to compare one passage with another or to analyze the continuing significance of biblical thought for the present day.

The questions rest on the theory that a student learns best, especially in the analysis of primary sources, when he examines material, finds significant information, and forms his own conclusions concerning the thought of the writers and the methods of biblical study. Although this inductive method may require more preparation on the part of the student than other types of teaching, it establishes a procedure that the student can continue to use independently in further study of the Bible or other source materials.

The guide is designed primarily for introductory courses in colleges and seminaries, although it could also be used by groups such as adult study classes in churches. It is intended to supplement, rather than replace, introductory textbooks on the Old and New Testaments.

The individual topics are arranged in an approximate chronological order corresponding to the persons or events that are treated. The division into topics allows a considerable degree of flexibility in using the guide: the teacher can rearrange the order of the topics, devote several class periods to longer topics, or combine short topics into a single period.

Philip B. Harner
Department of Religion
Heidelberg College

PART ONE: THE OLD TESTAMENT

1.   Israel and the Ancient Near East

The "comparative religion" approach to Old Testament study examines similarities and differences
between the religion of Israel and other religions of
the Ancient Near East.   Sometimes the Israelites
rejected beliefs or practices of other religions.
Sometimes they took them over and modified them to fit
into the structure of their own faith.

1.   The Babylonian creation story comes from Meso-
     potamia, about 1800 B.C.   In the story Marduk, the
     lord of the gods, meets Tiamat, the goddess sea-
     monster, in single combat.   He slays her and splits
     her body into two parts.   With one part he makes
     the sky, the vault of heaven.   Then he creates the
     dry land, and the stars, planets, and moon.
     Another god then creates man from the blood of
     Kingu, Tiamat's consort, to perform menial services
     for the gods.

     In this story Tiamat represents the unruly, chaotic
     waters of the primordial ocean.   The Hebrew word
     tehom is probably related linguistically to the
     name Tiamat.

     Do you find any similarities between this story and
     the creation account in Gen. 1:1-2:4a?   Note that
     "deep" is tehom.   Do you find any differences?
     Does the Genesis account involve a combat between
     gods?   What is the role of man in the two accounts?

     For the idea of creation as combat, see Is. 51:9-10;
     Job 9:8;   Ps. 74:13; 89:9-10.   Do you think the Old
     Testament writers understood this idea literally
     or poetically?   If the latter, why do you think
     they used this language?

2.   The Nuzi tablets reflect practices in society in
     upper Mesopotamia in the 15th century B.C.   One of
     these customs was that an adopted son would have to
     give way to a real son as chief heir.   In light of

this, read Gen. 15:1-6. Who was Abraham's heir at this time? What was Abraham promised?

Another custom reflected in the Nuzi tablets was that a childless wife must provide her husband with a handmaid to bear children and thus maintain the family line. How is this custom reflected in Gen. 16:1-4; 30:1-5?

3. The Ras Shamra tablets come from Ugarit, in Syria, in the 15th and 14th centuries B.C. They reflect many religious beliefs and practices that were common along the eastern Mediterranean coast. One of these practices was that a young goat was boiled in its mother's milk as a magical rite to bring rain. According to Ex. 23:19b, what was the attitude of the Israelites toward this practice? Why do you think they took this attitude?

Prominent divinities in the Ras Shamra tablets were Baal, the god of the storm, rain, and fertility; and Anath, his sister, a warrior goddess. In the myths, Baal contends with Mot (death), the god of the rainless season. Baal is unable to overcome Mot and dies. Anath, mourning for Baal, kills or subdues Mot. Baal returns to life, and Mot also regains his powers. They fight again, but inconclusively - i.e., neither of the contending forces, fertility or sterility, could be eliminated from the cycle of the seasons.

When the Israelites entered Canaan, they found that the native Canaanites practiced this type of Baal worship. The worship of Baal was a practical religion for an agricultural people, intended to insure that the fertile, growing season would return each year.

In light of this background, read Hos. 2:8-13; 11:1-4. Why does Hosea criticize the Israelites? Why do you think they were attracted to Baal worship?

4. The Egyptian pharaoh Akhnaton, who ruled from 1370-1353 B.C., brought about a short-lived religious revolution in Egypt by introducing the monotheistic worship of the sun (the Aton). The Hymn to the Aton, attributed to him, praises the sun as the sole god, beneficent and universal, creating the world.

The Hymn to the Aton shows some similarity to Ps.
104. Do you see any difference in the way this
psalm depicts God?

5. The pharaoh of Egypt was an absolute monarch, and
the kings of other countries in the Ancient Near
East enjoyed extensive power. The Israelites were
reluctant at first to establish a monarchy. What
early attitude does Gideon express, in Judg. 8:22-
23? What attitude is reflected by Jotham's
parable, in Judg. 9:7-15?

When the Israelites did form a monarchy, how did
they understand the power of the king, according to
Ps. 89:19-37? What limitations did they place on
kingship, according to Deut. 17:14-20?

6. About 540 B.C., Second Isaiah, one of the Jewish
exiles in Babylon, wrote about the imminent down-
fall of Babylon. He mentions two important
Babylonian gods, Bel and Nebo. How does he
contrast them with his own God, Yahweh, in Is. 46:
1-4?

    2. Traditions of Israel's Faith

    Most of the themes or traditions of Israel's
faith had their basis in historical events. The method
of "tradition criticism" examines the way these
traditions were handed down from generation to generation, related to one another, and applied to current
situations in the life of the people.

1. The most familiar accounts of creation are Gen.
1:1-2:4a and Gen. 2:4b-3:24.

A poetic description of creation occurs in Ps. 74:
12-17. Why do you think the writer uses the word
"salvation" in vs. 12? The Hebrew word is
yeshuoth, plural of yeshuah; the plural could be
translated "deeds of salvation."

In Is. 40:27-31, Second Isaiah refers to the Lord
(Yahweh) as the creator of the earth. Why do you

think he refers to Yahweh in this way – i.e., how does creation faith function in this passage?

2. The patriarchal tradition refers to events connected with Abraham (about 1750 B.C.), Isaac, and Jacob. According to Gen. 12:1-3, Yahweh made several promises to Abraham when he was still in northern Mesopotamia. What were these promises? What do they suggest about Yahweh? What do they suggest that Abraham will need?

   About 540 B.C., Second Isaiah was one of the Jewish exiles in Mesopotamia. Why do you think he referred to Abraham, in Is. 51:1-3?

3. The Exodus tradition refers to the time of Moses, about 1290 B.C., when the Israelites escaped from slavery in Egypt. A brief reference to the Exodus occurs in Ex. 3:7-8. What is the nature of Yahweh, according to this passage?

   In Amos 3:102, Amos refers to the Exodus from Egypt. How does he understand the meaning of the Exodus tradition for his own day? Does it signify special privilege or special responsibility for Israel?

   In Hos. 11:1-2, Hosea also refers to the Exodus. What contrast does he seek to bring out?

   In Is. 51:10b-11, Second Isaiah refers to the Exodus. What does this reference mean to him?

4. The wilderness tradition refers to the period of forty years when the Israelites wandered in the Sinai peninsula, after the Exodus from Egypt. Ex. 16:1-30 describes some events that occurred during this time. How does this passage depict Yahweh? How does it describe the Israelites?

5. The Sinai covenant tradition refers to the covenant that God made with the Israelites at Mt. Sinai during their stay in the wilderness. The basic account is in Ex. 20:1-17. What do you think is the significance of the reference to the Exodus in vs. 2? Why do you think the first commandment (vs. 3) is placed first?

   According to Hos. 4:1-3, did Hosea think the people of his day were obeying the Sinai covenant?

According to Jer. 11:1-13, did Jeremiah think the people were keeping the covenant?

6. The conquest tradition refers to the Israelite conquest of the land of Canaan, about 1250-1200 B.C., after the stay in the wilderness. A reference to the conquest occurs in Deut. 6:10-15. How is the conquest connected here with the patriarchal tradition? What is the conquest to mean to the Israelites? How would you apply this passage to American history?

7. The Davidic tradition refers to the special covenant that Yahweh made with king David and his descendants on the throne in Jerusalem. According to II Sam. 7:1-17, what did Yahweh promise to David? In what way do you think the Sinai covenant has influenced the Davidic covenant here?

8. The Zion tradition expresses the belief that Yahweh will protect his city, Jerusalem, and especially the temple. Note how Ps. 48 reflects this belief. According to Is. 31:4-5, did Isaiah utilize this tradition? According to Micah 3:9-12, did Micah subscribe to it?

9. Short summaries of traditions occur occasionally in the Old Testament. Analyze the following passages: Deut. 26:5-10; Ps. 136; Neh. 9:6-37. What traditions does each passage include? Can you think of any reasons why some traditions are omitted?

If an ancient Israelite were asked to "define" God, he would probably reply in terms of short summaries such as those above. What would this indicate about the Israelite understanding of God? How would it differ from the attitude of Aristotle, who defined God in terms such as the unmoved mover and the first cause?

3. The Creation of the World

The creation account in Gen. 1:1–2:4a is often regarded as part of the priestly document (P), written about 550 B.C. The account of creation and the garden of Eden in Gen. 2:4b–3:24 is often regarded as part of the earlier Yahwist document (J), written about 950 B.C.

1. Each item in the following list describes one of these accounts. Place a "P" or a "J" after each item to show which account it describes.

    a. solemn, majestic prose style
    b. simple, flowing, narrative style
    c. God referred to mostly as "Lord God"
    d. God referred to throughout as "God"
    e. complex cosmology: dry land, solid firmament, waters above the firmament and below the earth
    f. simpler cosmology: earth apparently a dry plain, with springs or lakes
    g. verbs describing God's work: "created," "made," "separated"
    h. verbs describing God's work: "made," "formed"
    i. man created first, before other living things
    j. man created last, after other living things
    k. sabbath rest based in creation itself
    l. division into days
    m. man and woman created at the same time
    n. man created first, then woman
    o. structure of command ("God said"), fulfillment ("and it was so"), and response ("God saw that it was good")
    p. emphasis on orderliness of creation and proper place of each thing in creation
    q. emphasis on man's relationship with other beings and with God, the meaning of work, the nature of freedom
    r. emphasis on man's role as crown of creation

2. In contrast to the question above, which examines differences between the two accounts, what ideas about God do both accounts express? What ideas about man do they both express?

3. What do you think is meant by the seven "days" of the P account? Would you regard this account as consistent or inconsistent with the theory of evolution? Explain.

4. Could God create light (Gen. 1:3-5) before he created the sun (Gen. 1:14-18)?

5. In Babylonian religion the sun, moon, and stars were regarded as divinities that could influence events on earth. What is their function according to Gen. 1:14-18? Do you think the writer of this passage was intentionally trying to correct the beliefs of Babylonian religion? Why?

6. What do you think is meant by the word "us" in Gen. 1:26? Cf. Ps. 82:1; 138:1.

7. What do you think is meant by the "image" of God in Gen. 1:26?

8. What do you think is meant by "dominion" over the earth, in Gen. 1:26, 28? Is man's dominion consistent with the modern interest in ecology?

9. According to the Greek philosopher Plato, man consists of an immortal soul temporarily placed in a mortal body. How would you compare this idea with the view of human nature in Gen. 2:7?

10. What different views of work are reflected in Gen. 2:15 and Gen. 3:17-19? Do you think both views are applicable today?

11. Why do you think God commanded man not to eat from "the tree of the knowledge of good and evil" in Gen. 2:17?

4. Primordial History

Interpreters differ concerning the historicity of the events described in Gen. 3-11. Some regard them as actual events. Others regard them as myths and legends which are "true" in the sense that they convey important religious truths about human life. In terms of the documentary theory, the material in these

7

chapters comes from J and P. J speaks of "the Lord," and P speaks of "God."

1. The J material in these chapters includes four main sections: the garden of Eden, Cain and Abel, the flood, and the tower of Babel. The garden of Eden is depicted in Gen. 3. The J writer describes three major events in this scene: a) man does something wrong; b) God punishes the wrongdoing; c) God shows his mercy in some way, so that the relationship between himself and man is not completely broken. Can you identify each of these events in Gen. 3?

2. In its earliest form the story about Cain and Abel, in Gen. 4:1-16, may have expressed the enmity between farmer and nomad. The J writer uses it to depict the same sequence of events as above: wrongdoing, punishment, and mercy. What form does each of these take in this account?

3. The flood story weaves together material from J and P. J material is found in Gen. 6:5-8; 7:1-5; 8:6-12, 20-22. The same sequence of events occurs here as in the accounts above. What form do they take?

4. The incident of the tower of Babel occurs in Gen. 11:1-9. In what way does it illustrate the theme of wrongdoing? How does it understand punishment? The theme of mercy does not appear in this section; the J writer, however, presents this theme in Gen. 12:1-3.

5. In these accounts (questions 1-4) the J writer is expressing his understanding of human life in general (apart from Yahweh's redemptive action through the patriarchs and Israel). How would you describe his understanding of human life? Do you think it applies today?

6. After its account of the flood, the P document describes a covenant that God made (Gen. 9:1-17). With whom did God make the covenant? What was its content? What is the sign or symbol of this covenant?

7. The idea that man is created in the "image" of God appears only in the P document in the Old Testament.

Note that man is made in the image of God before the flood (Gen. 1:26-27) and also after the flood (Gen. 9:6). What do you think it means that man is still in the image of God?

5. Abraham

The patriarchs were Hebrews, or "wanderers," who lived a nomadic life in Canaan. They were the ancestors of the Israelites and also of other peoples who lived near Canaan. Abraham, the first patriarch, probably lived about 1750 B.C., during the Middle Bronze Age.

1. Gen. 11:27-32 gives the background to Abraham's journeys. From what city did he start out? Where did he settle for a time? ("Abram" is Abraham.)

2. Gen. 12:1-9 continues the story of Abraham's journeys. What promises did God make to him? What did he do in response?

3. Gen. 12:10-20 tells of a brief visit to Egypt. When there was a famine in Canaan, why do you think people would go to Egypt? Do you think Abraham dealt fairly with his wife, Sarah (Sarai)? Can you relate this incident to any of the promises mentioned in Gen. 12:1-3? Why do you think the Old Testament writers included this incident?

4. Why did Abraham and Lot separate, in Gen. 13:1-12? What areas did each take? How could Lot's decision have threatened God's covenant with Abraham? What does this incident reveal about Abraham?

5. Gen. 16:1-16 tells of the birth of Ishmael (cf. Topic 1, question 2). Gen. 21:1-21 gives the continuation of the story, telling of the birth of Isaac. How do Sarah and Hagar treat each other? What status does God give to Isaac? What provision does God make for Ishmael?

6. Gen. 22:1-19 tells of the near-sacrifice of Isaac. What does this passage tell about Yahweh and human sacrifice? About Yahweh and his covenant with Abraham? About the meaning of sacrifice? About

the character of Abraham?

7. According to a study by Albrecht Alt, the native inhabitants of Canaan at this time believed in deities who were restricted to local sanctuaries, so that people had to go to these sanctuaries to worship them. From your study of God's dealings with Abraham, how would you say God differed from these local deities?

8. The Genesis accounts say relatively little about Isaac. However, compare Gen. 12:1-3 with Gen. 26:1-5. Does God make the same promises to Isaac that he made to Abraham?

6. Jacob

Esau and Jacob - the sons of Isaac and Rebekah - were twins, although Esau was first-born and thus the elder. Esau was regarded as the ancestor of Edom, a country to the south of Canaan. Jacob, through his twelve sons, was considered the ancestor of the tribes of Israel. This connection is indicated in Gen. 32:28, when Jacob's name is changed to Israel (the first time the word Israel occurs in the Old Testament).

1. Gen. 25:29-34 tells how Jacob "bought" the birthright from Esau. The birthright of the elder son signified a double share in the family inheritance. Do you think it means anything more here, in the sense that Esau symbolizes Edom, and Jacob symbolizes Israel?

2. A deathbed blessing was considered especially efficacious, and it could not be retracted. In Gen. 27:1-46, how does Jacob manage to obtain Isaac's blessing? What role does Rebekah play? What did the blessing signify about the future relations between Jacob and Esau? What did Rebekah advise Jacob to do after receiving the blessing?

3. As Jacob starts his journey, he comes to Bethel, in central Canaan (Gen. 28:1-22). What happened to him there? Did he receive the same promises that had

been given to Abraham (Gen. 12:1-3)?

4. Gen. 29:1-30 begins the story of Jacob's stay in Haran, at the home of Laban, his uncle. How did Jacob meet his wife Rachel? How many years did he serve for her?

5. According to Gen. 30:25-43, how did Laban try to cheat Jacob? What did Jacob do in return?

6. When Jacob leaves Haran, how does he justify himself to Laban? What was the original significance of the "Mizpah benediction" (Gen. 31:36-54)?

7. Gen. 32:1-33:20 tells how Jacob returned to Canaan after an absence of twenty years. What did he do to avert the anger of his brother Esau? How did Esau treat him? Does Gen. 33:4 remind you of a particular parable in the New Testament?

7. Joseph

Joseph, one of the sons of Jacob, may be regarded as a transitional link between the patriarchal period and the later time of Moses. Joseph went to Egypt, probably about 1720 B.C. He rose to prominence and was eventually reunited with his brothers, who also went there to live. According to Ex. 12:40, the Hebrews lived in Egypt 430 years.

1. Gen. 37:1-36 begins the story of Joseph. Why did Jacob (Israel) love Joseph more than his other children? What did Joseph's dreams mean? Do you think his brothers were justified in their actions? How would you explain the confusing roles of the Ishmaelites and the Midianites in Gen. 37:27-28, 36?

2. Gen. 39:1-23 tells the story of Joseph and Potiphar's wife. Apart from the surface theme (the false charge against Joseph), what do you think is the underlying theme of the chapter?

3. Gen. 40:1-23 relates an incident that occurred while Joseph was in prison. What is the pun which

11

expresses the point of the story?

4. According to Gen. 41:1-57, what dreams did the
    pharaoh have? How did Joseph interpret them?
    What happened to Joseph as a result? Did the
    dreams come true?

5. Gen. 42:1-46:7 tells how Joseph's brothers came to
    Egypt. Why did Joseph especially ask for Benjamin
    to come? Why did he put the money and the silver
    cup in his brothers' sacks of grain? Why did he
    not identify himself until 45:3? What do you think
    is the significance of Gen. 46:4, in relation to
    Gen. 12:1-3?

6. What is the theme of the Joseph cycle, according to
    Gen. 45:5-8; 50:20-21?

8. The Exodus from Egypt

The Exodus from Egypt probably occurred about
1290 B.C., when Rameses II was pharaoh. Although it is
uncertain exactly when, where, or how the Israelites
crossed the "sea" to escape from Egypt, they understood
the Exodus as a wonderful event in which Yahweh
delivered them from slavery.

1. Ex. 1:1-22 summarizes very briefly the centuries
    from Joseph to Moses. The "new king" who oppressed
    the Hebrews may have been Ahmose I, about 1570 B.C.
    What did the Hebrews have to do for the Egyptians?

2. Ex. 2:1-25 tells of the childhood and early life of
    Moses. How did it happen that he grew up in the
    Egyptian court? Why did he leave Egypt?

3. In Ex. 3:1-22, Moses meets God in the burning bush.
    What does this incident reveal about the nature of
    God? Who takes the initiative in planning the
    Exodus? How would you explain the meaning of the
    name Yahweh, according to Ex. 3:13-15?

4. According to Adolf Deissmann, religious experience
    may be "ascending" (in which man finds the way to
    God) or "descending" (in which God comes to man).

It may result in "union" (in which the human merges
with the divine) or "communion" (in which man has
fellowship with God). Which of these terms do you
think apply to Moses' experience in Ex. 3?

5. In Ex. 6:2-9, how is the time of the Exodus linked
to the earlier patriarchal period?

6. Compare Gen. 4:26 (from the J document), Ex. 3:13-
15 (from the E document), and Ex. 6:2-3 (from the
P document). How do the documents deal with the
question when God became known by his special name,
Yahweh? Can you think of any explanation for this
difference?

7. Ex. 7:1-24 describes the first plagues that
afflicted Egypt. What role does Aaron have here?
What is the purpose of the plagues? Do they
achieve this purpose?

8. Why did God "harden Pharaoh's heart" (Ex. 7:3; 9:12;
10:1, 20, 27; 11:10; 14:4)? What do you think this
expression means? Why do the accounts also say
that Pharaoh hardened his own heart (Ex. 8:15, 32;
9:34)? How would you relate these two ideas to
each other?

9. What was the origin of the festival of Passover,
according to Ex. 12:1-39? Why did the people eat
unleavened bread? How many Israelites left Egypt?

10. Ex. 14:1-31 describes the crossing of the "sea" or
the "sea of reeds" (yam suph, Ex. 13:18; 15:4).
Describe briefly in your own words what happened.

9. The Wanderings in the Wilderness

The Israelites spent forty years, approximately
1290-1250 B.C., in the wilderness of the Sinai
peninsula. They spent much of this time in or near
Kadesh, an oasis area in the northeastern part of the
peninsula.

1. Ex. 16:1-17:7 describes some events that occurred
soon after the people left Egypt. Why did they

13

"murmur" or complain? Did they prefer security or freedom? How did God provide them with food and water? What special observance was instituted at this time?

2. According to Ex. 18:1-27, Jethro, the father-in-law of Moses, visited Moses. How did he react to hearing news of the Exodus? What administrative advice did he give Moses?

3. According to Ex. 32:1-24, the people made a golden calf while Moses was on Mt. Sinai. Why did they do this? What was Aaron's role? How did Moses persuade God not to destroy the people? What does this incident reveal about God's way of working with his people? Is it similar in any way to the patriarchal narratives?

4. According to Ex. 33:7-23, whom did Moses "meet" at the tent of meeting? What did God promise Moses on this occasion? In what way were the people of Israel "distinct" from other peoples? Is Ex. 33:11 consistent with Ex. 33:18-23? What do you think each of these passages is trying to express?

5. Note the "Aaronic benediction" in Num. 6:22-27.

6. According to Num. 11:1-35, what were the people still doing? How did Moses feel? What two measures did God take to deal with the situation?

7. Num. 13:1-14:45 describes a spying expedition from Kadesh into southern Canaan. Did the spies find this part of Canaan prosperous? Did they find it well fortified? How did the people react? How did Joshua and Caleb react? When the people did decide to invade southern Canaan, were they successful?

8. According to Num. 20:1-13, what mistake did Moses make? What was the consequence?

10. The Sinai Covenant

After they escaped from Egypt, the Israelite people received a covenant from Yahweh at Mt. Sinai. As the Exodus revealed Yahweh's gracious concern for

14

his people, the Sinai covenant formalized their relationship with him and established the norms for their religious and social life. The Ten Commandments are the basic part of the Sinai covenant, although other laws and regulations are also connected with it in the Old Testament accounts.

1. Ex. 19:1-6 gives a "preview" of the Sinai Covenant. What is Yahweh's part, according to vs. 4? What is the people's part, according to vs. 5? How do you think all the people can be a "kingdom of priests"?

2. Some scholars find parallels between the Hittite treaties and the Sinai covenant. The Hittites lived in central Turkey, about 1400-1200 B.C., and made suzerainty treaties with nearby countries. In these treaties the Hittite king a) identifies himself, b) tells what he has done in the past for the recipient, and c) gives treaty stipulations that the recipient must adhere to. Can you find parallels to these three themes in Ex. 20:1-17? What do these parallels suggest about the relation between "grace" and "law" in Old Testament thought? What do they suggest about the role of gratitude to God as a reason for obeying his commandments?

3. Some of the stipulations in the Hittite treaties were that the recipient must not make similar treaties with other countries, and he must remain on good terms with other countries that have similar treaties with the Hittites. Can you find parallels to these stipulations in Ex. 20:3-17?

4. Does the first commandment (Ex. 20:3) reflect a belief in polytheism (many gods for one people), henotheism (one God for the Israelites, other gods for other peoples), or monotheism (only one God over all the earth)? What belief is expressed in Is. 43:10-11; 44:6?

5. If a recipient of a treaty from the Hittites broke the treaty, then he, his household, his son, and his grandson would be punished. How would you compare this with Ex. 20:5?

6. Why should the Israelites observe the sabbath, according to Ex. 20:5-11? Is the same reason given in Deut. 5:12-15?

7. How would you interpret the prohibition against killing, in view of the fact that the Israelites engaged in warfare with other peoples and also established capital punishment for some offenses?

8. The Ten Commandments are part of the Sinai covenant, made with the whole people of Israel. Yet the commandments themselves are in the singular ("thou shalt..."). Why is it significant that they are addressed to individual persons?

9. Most of the Ten Commandments are negative in form, indicating what the people should not do. Do you think that this form of commandment gives the people more freedom, or less, in arranging their lives?

10. Ex. 24:3-8 describes a ceremony by which the Sinai covenant was ratified. What are the people asked to do? What does Moses do with the blood from the sacrifices? What does this signify?

11. To what extent do you think the Ten Commandments are observed in the United States today? In view of the principle of separation between church and state, to what extent should government try to enforce them?

12. Ex. 21:23-25 states the lex talionis, the law of retaliation. According to some interpreters, this principle represented an advance in morality at that time. Can you explain what this means?

13. According to Ex. 22:21-24, how were the Israelites to treat strangers, widows, and orphans? According to Ex. 23:10-11, what were they to do for the poor?

14. What regulations concerning money-lending did the Israelites have, according to Ex. 22:25-27?

15. How were the Israelites to treat their enemies, according to Ex. 23:4-5?

16. What standards of judicial administration did the Israelites have, according to Ex. 23:6-8?

11. The Conquest of Canaan

After their stay in the wilderness the Israelites finally entered Canaan, about 1250-1200 B.C. Wending their way around the Salt Sea, they entered the country from the east and settled initially in the less densely inhabited areas. (Reading: Josh. 1-12; 24. Judg. 1:1-2:5.)

1. When the Israelites first escaped from Egypt, why did they not go directly to Canaan by the road that ran along the Mediterranean Sea? Cf. Ex. 13:17.

2. When the Israelites were at Kadesh, why did they not enter Canaan directly from the south? Cf. Num. 14:39-45; also Topic 9, question 7.

3. Where did Moses die? Who succeeded him? Cf. Deut. 34:1-12.

4. What did God promise Joshua, in Josh. 1:1-9? What was Joshua to do?

5. According to the book of Joshua, the Israelites conquered Canaan in three swift campaigns. The first, in the center of the land, involved the crossing of the Jordan River and the destruction of Jericho and Ai (Josh. 2-8). To what earlier event was the crossing of the Jordan compared (Josh. 3-4)? Why did the Israelites set up twelve stones?

6. How did the Israelites destroy Jericho, according to Josh. 6? What did they do to the inhabitants? Why?

7. Who was Achan, according to Josh. 7? What did he do? How was he punished? Who was punished with him? Cf. Deut. 24:16; Jer. 31:29-30; Ezek. 18:1-4. Do these passages reflect a different view of punishment?

8. How did the Israelites conquer Ai, according to Josh. 8?

9. In the second campaign, according to the book of Joshua, the Israelites made a treaty with the Gibeonites, defeated a coalition of Canaanite

chieftains, and took a number of cities in the
southern part of Canaan (Josh. 9-10). Why did the
Gibeonites want to make a treaty with the
Israelites? How did they trick them? Did the
Israelites honor the treaty?

10. According to the third campaign, Joshua destroyed
Hazor, in the northern part of the country (Josh.
11). Does the summary in Josh. 11:23 suggest that
the conquest was complete at this time?

11. The accounts of the conquest in Josh. 1-12 do not
mention any battles in the north-central part of
Canaan, around Shechem. Josh. 24:1-28, however,
describes a ceremony of covenant renewal at Shechem.
Some interpreters have suggested that the inhabitants of this area were also invited to join the
covenant and worship Yahweh at this time. Do you
find any evidence in Josh. 24:1-28 to support this
view?

12. Archaeological findings indicate that some Canaanite
cities (Bethel, Eglon, Debir, Lachish, Hazor) did
suffer destruction in the latter part of the
thirteenth century B.C. On the other hand, Jericho
was a small settlement or uninhabited at this time,
and Ai ("ruin") had been in ruins for about a
thousand years. How would you relate these findings
to the account of the conquest in Josh. 1-12?

13. According to Judg. 1:1-2:5, do the tribes of Israel
act together or individually in fighting the
Canaanites? Are they always successful? How would
you compare this account with Josh. 1-12?

12. The Period of the Judges

During the period 1200-1020 B.C. the Israelites
sought to strengthen their control over Canaan, defend
the land from external threats, and come to terms with
Canaanite culture and religion (cf. Topic 1, question
3). Not yet organized politically as a nation, they
existed as a loose confederation of tribes held together
by their covenant allegiance to Yahweh. Since there was
no professional army, leaders known as "judges" rose up
in times of emergency to lead the people in defending

their land. (Reading: Judg. 2:6-16:31).

1. The book of Judges was edited in the sixth century
B.C. by a Deuteronomic historian who sought to
interpret this early period in terms of cycles of
apostasy, punishment, penitence, and deliverance.
This viewpoint is presented in Judg. 2:11-23 and
also, more clearly, in the story of Othniel in
Judg. 3:7-11. Can you explain what each of these
terms means?

2. To what extent do you think the Deuteronomic interpretation of history is accurate? Can you compare
it with other ways of interpreting history? Do you
think it applies in every situation?

3. From whom did Ehud deliver the Israelites (Judg.
3:12-30)? How did he do this?

4. Judg. 4 and 5 are parallel accounts of Deborah and
the battle of Mediggo. Which one is in prose?
Which one is in poetry? Which do you think is
earlier? How did Sisera die, in each account?
According to Judg. 5, did all the Israelite tribes
join in the battle?

5. What was Gideon's occupation? Why was he afraid to
tear down the altar of Baal (Judg. 6)? How did he
select the 300 men who were to fight the Midianites
(Judg. 7)? What did he say when he was offered the
opportunity to become king (Judg. 8)? Why?

6. Abimelech was not really a judge, for he did not
deliver Israel from any enemy. A son of Gideon, he
established a brief, three-year reign over the city
of Shechem and its environs (Judg. 9). What view of
kingship does Jotham's parable express? What
happened to Abimelech?

7. From whom did Jephthah deliver the Israelites (Judg.
10:17-11:40)? What vow did he make? What happened
as a result? How would you compare this incident
with the story of Abraham and Isaac in Gen. 22?

8. Samson was a judge in the sense that he harassed
the Philistines by his exploits of strength (Judg.
13:1-16:31). What do we learn about the Philistines
from these stories? In what way did God make use of
Samson?

9. According to Judg. 10:10-16, what religious problem arose for the Israelites during this time? How did Yahweh remind them of their obligation to him?

13.   Samuel and Saul

Samuel lived in the closing years of the period of the Judges, when the Israelites were still threatened by enemies such as the Philistines and the Ammonites. Although the exact nature of his role is not clear, he was instrumental in the selection of Saul as the first king of Israel. Saul reigned for twenty years, from 1020 to 1000 B.C., spending most of his reign at war and finally losing his life in a battle with the Philistines. (Reading: I Sam. 1-12.)

1. I Sam. 1 describes how an Israelite family, toward the end of the period of the Judges, went to worship at Shiloh. Describe these visits on the basis of this chapter. Who went, and how often? What did they do there? Who was in charge at Shiloh? How was Yahweh's presence represented there, according to I Sam. 3:3?

2. Compare Hannah's prayer (I Sam. 2:1-10) with the "Magnificat" in Lk. 1:46-55. What ideas occur in both passages? Compare also I Sam. 2:26 with Lk. 2:52.

3. I Sam. 2:27-36 describes how a "man of God" says that the priesthood will pass from Eli's house to another priestly house. Analyze the main ideas in the man's speech. What ideas occur before the word "therefore" in vs. 30? What ideas occur after this word?

4. What happened to the Philistines when they captured the ark of Yahweh (I Sam. 5)? What did the Philistines do with the ark (I Sam. 6)? What were the five cities of the Philistines (I Sam. 6:17)? What happened to the Israelites when they looked into the ark (I Sam. 6:19)? Can you think of any explanation for this?

5. According to one theory, two separate accounts have

been combined in I Sam. 7-12 to describe the selection of Saul as king. Read the "Saul Source" first as a connected account: I Sam. 9:1-10:16; 11:1-15. Why does Saul go to Zuph, about 25 miles northwest of Jerusalem (I Sam. 9)? What terms are used to describe Samuel? What does Yahweh tell Samuel to do? Where does Samuel anoint Saul as prince over Israel (I Sam. 10:1-16)? Where do all the people make Saul king (I Sam. 11:1-15)?

6. Next read the "Samuel Source" as a connected account: I Sam. 7:3-8:22; 10:17-27; 12:1-25. What functions does Samuel have (I Sam. 7)? Who takes the initiative in asking for a king (I Sam. 8)? Why? Does Samuel approve? Does Yahweh approve? How does Samuel describe their existence under a king? Where is Saul chosen as king (I Sam. 10:17-27)?

7. If there are two different accounts of the founding of the monarchy in I Sam. 7-12, how do you think they arose? Why do you think later editors included them both?

8. Compare I Sam. 8:10-18 with the following passages, which describe conditions later under king Solomon: I Kings 4:1-7; 5:13-14; 9:20-22.

9. What are the four parts of the Deuteronomic interpretation of history (cf. Topic 12, question 1)? Can you find these four themes in Samuel's speech in I Sam. 12:6-11?

10. What is the difference between a covenant people and a nation? How does Samuel attempt to combine these two ideas in his speech in I Sam. 12:12-25? Can Americans in a similar way understand themselves today as a religious people and a nation?

11. When Israel made the transition from tribal confederation to monarchy, what did it gain? What did it lose?

14. David

David, who ruled Israel from 1000 to 961 B.C., brought political stability to the new nation by confining the Philistines to the coastal plain, incorporating the areas of the old Canaanite city-states into Israelite territory, and subjugating a number of neighboring countries. At the same time that new religious ideas were being introduced, he sought to preserve early traditions from the time of Moses by bringing the ark into Jerusalem. In later centuries the Israelites looked back to the reign of David as a kind of golden age.

1. The familiar story of David and Goliath is told in I Sam. 17:1-58. Why is it significant that Goliath was a Philistine? To whom did David attribute his victory (I Sam. 17:45-47)?

2. For another reference to Goliath, see II Sam. 21:19; cf. also the notice in I Chron. 20:5, which was written much later. Can you think of any reason for these different accounts?

3. According to II Sam. 2:1-4, where did David first become king? Over what part of the country? According to II Sam. 5:1-5, who else asked David to be their king? If David became king over the whole country in two separate stages, what do you think he would have to be careful to do?

4. Why was Jerusalem known as the city of David, according to II Sam. 5:6-10? Why was it a good site for his capital?

5. Where did David install the ark, according to II Sam. 6:1-15? Why do you think he did this? For the incident concerning Uzzah, cf. Topic 13, question 4.

6. II Sam. 7:1-29 describes the beginning of the "royal theology" or the Davidic covenant. What does David want to do? What are the two meanings of the word "house" in this passage? What promises does Yahweh make to David?

7. What were some of David's military accomplishments,

according to II Sam. 8:1-18?

8. Which two of the Ten Commandments did David violate, according to II Sam. 11? What was the point of Nathan's parable in II Sam. 12? What effect did it have on David? How does this incident illustrate the relationship between the Davidic covenant and the Sinai covenant? On what did the prophet Nathan base his authority?

9. According to II Sam. 15, how did Absalom seek to replace his father (David) on the throne? Why do you think he went to Hebron? When David fled from Jerusalem, how did he arrange to receive information?

10. When David's army fought to regain his throne, what instructions did he give concerning Absalom (II Sam. 18)? What happened? How did David react?

15. Solomon

Solomon ruled from 961 to 922 B.C. Since peace prevailed throughout most of his reign, he emphasized the economic and commercial development of the nation. Among his building projects were the Jerusalem temple and the royal palace. (Reading: I Kings 1-12.)

1. What did Solomon pray for, according to I Kings 3:1-15? How did Yahweh answer his prayer?

2. How did Solomon adjudicate the quarrel of the two women, according to I Kings 3:16-28?

3. I Kings 6:1-38 describes the Jerusalem temple that Solomon built. How large was the temple? What building materials were used? What were the three main parts of the temple? What was in the inner sanctuary?

4. I Kings 8:1-21 describes how the priests brought the ark into the new temple. What was in the ark?

5. I Kings 8:22-66 gives Solomon's prayer at the dedication of the temple. According to this prayer,

where does God dwell? If God does not dwell in the temple, what is the function of the temple? Can non-Israelites pray at the temple?

6. Compare the descriptions of the forced labor which Solomon levied in I Kings 5:13-14 and 9:15-22. Can you determine whether or not Solomon used Israelites for this forced labor?

7. How would you describe conditions in Solomon's court, according to I Kings 4:7, 22-28; 10:14-27? What commercial activities did Solomon engage in according to I Kings 9:26-28; 10:22, 28-29?

8. What was the result of Solomon's many marriages, according to I Kings 11:1-13? What did Yahweh do?

9. According to I Kings 11:26-12:24, who succeeded Solomon in Judah? Who succeeded him in Israel? Why did Israel break away and choose its own king? Cf. Topic 14, question 3.

10. What similarities and differences can you find between Moses and Solomon?

16.   The J Document

        According to the documentary hypothesis, the first five books of the Old Testament consist of four documents, known as J, E, D, and P. The earliest of these, the J document, may have been composed about 950 B.C., during the reign of Solomon. The anonymous author is known as the Yahwist because of his use of the divine name Yahweh. The three main divisions of the J document deal with the primordial history, the patriarchs, and the time of Moses.

1. According to the Yahwist, when did people come to know God by his special name, Yahweh (Gen. 4:26)? What conviction does the Yahwist express by introducing the name at this point?

2. Review Topic 4, questions 1-5. As the Yahwist looks at human life in general, would you say that he is optimistic or pessimistic? Why?

24

3. What attitude toward work does the Yahwist reflect in Gen. 2:15? In Gen. 3:17-19? How does this compare with the attitude that is suggested in Eccles. 2:11, 18-24? Can you relate these ideas to people's attitudes toward work today?

4. The Yahwist uses anthropomorphic language (human terms) to describe God. For example, God walks in the garden and speaks to man (Gen. 3:8-9). Why do you think he uses such language? Is it an appropriate or inappropriate way to speak of God? Do we ever use such language today?

5. Does the Yahwist have a critical attitude toward urban life? Cf. Gen. 4:17; 11:4. Why do you think he had this attitude?

6. According to the Yahwist, God's special redemptive work in history begins with the patriarchs, who are forerunners of Israel. Note the three promises (land, descendants, blessing) that God gives to Abraham in Gen. 12:1-3. How can all the people of the earth be blessed in Abraham?

7. The Yahwist tells the story of Abraham and Sarah (Gen. 12:10-20) without making any ethical judgment on Abraham's conduct. Why then do you think he includes the incident?

8. The J document provides much of the narrative material that tells of the Exodus from Egypt, the wandering in the wilderness, the Sinai covenant, and the initial phase of the conquest east of the Jordan river. Ex. 24:1-2, 9-11 is the J account of the ceremony ratifying the Sinai covenant. How would you compare it with the E account in Ex. 24:3-8?

9. If the documentary hypothesis is correct, the Yahwist was the first person to write down a connected account of Israel's early history. In light of the changes that had occurred under David and Solomon, why do you think he decided to do this? If he were living today, what do you think he would do?

10. According to the documentary theory, the E document was written about 750 B.C. Its author is known as the Elohist because he uses the word God (elohim)

for the time before Moses. Apparently the E document had no account of creation or primordial history but began directly with the patriarchs. How would you compare the Elohist and the Yahwist in this respect? How would you characterize the viewpoint of each writer?

11. Compare Gen. 12:10-20 (J) with Gen. 20:1-17 (E). How does the Elohist attempt to make some excuse for Abraham's conduct?

12. The Elohist avoids the anthropomorphic language of the Yahwist. How does the Elohist believe that God communicates with man, according to Gen. 20:3, 6; 21:17; 31:11?

13. The E document introduces the divine name Yahweh in Ex. 3:13-15. How does this differ from the view of the J document? Can you think of any explanation for this difference?

17. Elijah and Elisha

One of the earliest prophets, Elijah was active about 850 B.C. in the northern kingdom (Israel). The fact that he came from the remote area of Tishbe, east of the Jordan, may help to explain his interest in the formative traditions of Israelite faith and his critical attitude toward events during the reign of king Ahab. His prophetic successor was Elisha.

1. Whom did king Ahab marry, according to I Kings 16:29-33? Where was she from? What did Ahab do for her? What did she do to the prophets of Yahweh (I Kings 18:13)? Whom did she bring to the royal court in Samaria (I Kings 18:19)?

2. What did Elijah do for the widow of Zarephath and her son, according to I Kings 17:1-24? Was Zarephath in Israel? Could Yahweh be active outside Israel?

3. I Kings 18:1-46 describes the contest between Elijah and the prophets of Baal at Mt. Carmel. The present form of the narrative seems to combine

two earlier accounts, one dealing with the sending of fire, the other with the sending of rain. In either case, what decision does Elijah ask the people to make? Why? What does this incident suggest about the relation of Yahweh to nature?

4. I Kings 19:1-21 tells of Elijah's flight to Mt. Horeb (Sinai). Why did he flee from Jezebel? Why do you think he went to Horeb? What does it signify that Elijah heard Yahweh as a still, small voice, rather than in the wind, earthquake, or fire? Why was Elijah discouraged? How did Yahweh reassure him?

5. Review Topic 8, question 4. How would you compare Elijah's encounter with God (I Kings 19) with Moses' experience at the burning bush (Ex. 3)?

6. I Kings 21:1-29 relates the incident of Naboth's vineyard. What attitude did Naboth have toward the ownership of land? What attitude did Jezebel have? How would you explain this difference? Which attitude do you think is more common today?

7. How would you describe Ahab's actions in I Kings 21? Did he try to do what was right? How did he do wrong?

8. What similarities do you see between Nathan's parable (II Sam. 12) and the story of Naboth's vineyard? How does each incident reflect the influence of the Sinai covenant?

9. What did Elijah do for Elisha, according to II Kings 2:9-12? What happened to Elijah? To what expectation did this give rise at a later time (Mal. 4:5)? How is this reflected in the New Testament (Matt. 17:9-13)?

10. Compare I Kings 17:8-24 and II Kings 5:1-17 with Luke 4:25-28. What did Elijah and Elisha do? Why do you think Jesus referred to these events?

18. Amos

The first of the "writing prophets," Amos was
active about 750 B.C. in the northern kingdom. Perhaps
more than any other prophet, he emphasized that justice
and righteousness must be practiced in society as well
as in individual life. (Reading: Amos.)

1. Where was Amos from, according to 1:1? Who were
   the kings of Judah and Israel?

2. How did the priest Amaziah receive Amos at Bethel
   (7:10-17)? How did Amos react? Why did he reject
   the title of prophet? How does he describe
   himself? Why was there a sanctuary at Bethel
   (I Kings 12:26-29)?

3. Amos was especially concerned to apply the Exodus
   tradition to his own day. What meanings does he
   find in this tradition in 2:10; 3:1-2; 9:7? Do
   you think these meanings are still applicable
   today?

4. Analyze Amos' sermonette in 1:3-2:16. Under what
   conditions had the surrounding nations done wrong?
   Does Amos believe that Yahweh can punish these
   other nations? Under what conditions had Judah
   and Israel done wrong? How do you think the
   audience reacted up to 2:4? After 2:4? How would
   you state the main idea of this passage?

5. Sometimes Amos criticizes social conditions in
   Israel. Of what situations is he critical in 3:15;
   4:1; 6:4-7? Do you think these situations have a
   parallel in our own time?

6. Amos is also critical of economic practices in his
   society. What do you think he is referring to in
   2:6, 8; 8:4-6?

7. How does Amos criticize judicial practices in 5:10-
   12? The phrase "in the gate" refers to the administration of justice by elders in the village square.

8. Why does Amos criticize the religious life of the
   people, in 4:4-5; 5:21-24? Do you think that he
   wanted to abolish or reform public worship?

9. Note that questions 5 through 8 deal with social, economic, judicial, and religious conditions. In light of this, do you think Amos regarded religion as a separate compartment of life or a way of acting in all areas of life? Why?

10. In 5:1-2, Amos compares Israel to a young woman and composes a brief elegy in the poetic meter of a lament. What idea does he want to express?

11. In popular thought the "day of Yahweh" would be a time when God would vindicate and glorify his people. How does Amos treat this expectation in 5:18-20; 8:9-10?

12. What political events does Amos expect, according to 3:11; 6:7; 7:11; 9:4?

13. The three visions of 7:1-9 deal with punishments that God plans because of the people's transgressions. Why do you think Amos protests against the first two visions but not the third?

14. What is the meaning of the vision in 8:1-3? From the translation that you are using, can you find the play on words in this passage?

15. By criticizing the people for their wrongdoing, Amos usually uses an indirect way of expressing his understanding of God's will. Occasionally he states this understanding directly. According to 5:4, 6, 14-15, 24, what does Amos think the people should do?

16. According to 5:14-15; 7:1-6, does Amos have any hope that the people will change their ways so that God will not destroy them completely?

17. What kind of person do you think Amos was? Was he too harsh and severe? Was he too pessimistic? Explain your answer.

18. Some interpreters regard 9:8b-15 as a later addition to the book of Amos. Can you find any reasons for this view?

19. Hosea

Hosea was active in the northern kingdom (Israel). His career probably began during the last years of Jeroboam II (who died in 746 B.C.) and continued for some time into the turbulent period that followed, when Israel was threatened by the expansionist policies of Assyria. (Reading: Hosea.)

1. Hosea was married to a woman named Gomer, who had three children (1:2-8). The name of the first, Jezreel, represented a repudiation of the dynasty of Jehu in the northern kingdom, since Jehu had come to power about a century earlier by murdering potential rivals to the throne. What do the names of the other children signify? With Hosea 1:9, cf. Ex. 6:7.

2. Hosea went through four stages in his relationship with Gomer: he married Gomer (1:2-3), Gomer was unfaithful to him (2:5), Hosea divorced her (2:2, an ancient formula of divorce), Hosea found that he still loved Gomer and eventually restored her as his wife (3:1-3). Why do you think Hosea relates this experience, when otherwise he says almost nothing about himself?

3. Hosea then compared his marriage to Gomer with Yahweh's relationship to Israel, finding the same four stages: establishment of relationship, disruption of relationship, consequence of disruption, and renewal of relationship. Can you identify these four stages in 11:1-9? Who took the initiative in forming the relationship? When? Who was responsible for breaking the relationship? How? What consequence ensues? Why does Yahweh restore Israel as his covenant people?

4. Hosea had apparently passed through all four stages in his marriage to Gomer (question 2). How many stages had Yahweh's relation with Israel gone through (question 3)? How many were still to come?

5. What meaning does Hosea find in the tradition of the exodus from Egypt, according to 9:10; 11:1, 3-4; 13:4? How does he depict God in 11:1? How does he describe God in 13:4?

6. Who was Baal? Why would Israel regard Baal as the god who gave grain, wine, and oil (2:8)? According to Hosea, who actually gives the fruits of the earth?

7. According to 6:7, when did the Israelites begin to be unfaithful to their covenant with Yahweh? Note that Adam (Adamah) was a town on the Jordan river. "Transgressed" is a play on words; it also means "crossed over."

8. The passage in 4:1-3 uses the imagery of the law court; "controversy" can also be translated "lawsuit." Who is the plaintiff in this suit? Who is the defendant? What are the charges? What (implicitly) is the verdict? What is the consequence?

9. Note the charges in 4:1b. "Kindness" (RSV) is chesed, the idea of "steadfast love, covenant loyalty." Who is not loyal to the covenant? "Knowledge" may reflect the use of "know" in political treaties, in the sense of "recognize as a treaty partner." What does it mean to have "knowledge of God"?

10. Note the charges in 4:2. On what set of laws do you think they are based?

11. Compare the charges in 4:1b with those in 4:2. Which set is more general? Which is more specific? Which do you think underlies the other?

12. How would you summarize the underlying cause of the people's wrongdoing, according to 6:4, 6; 10:12; 13:4-6?

13. What does Hosea think of religious leaders such as priests and prophets, according to 4:4-6; 6:8-10; 9:7-9?

14. Review Topic 18, question 2, concerning Amos' visit to the state shrine at Bethel. What does Hosea think of this shrine, according to 8:5-6; 10:5-6? ("Bethaven" is used for "Bethel.")

15. What does Hosea think of political leaders such as the king and princes, according to 5:1-2; 7:1-7?

16. Review Topic 13, questions 5 and 6, concerning the

31

promonarchic "Saul Source" and the antimonarchic "Samuel Source." Which of these sources do you think Hosea would have agreed with, according to 8:4; 13:9-11?

17. What does Hosea think of reliance on military power and political alliances, according to 5:13-14; 7:11; 10:13-15; 12:1?

18. What does Hosea think of sacrifice, according to 6:6; 8:13? According to the Gospel of Matthew (9:13; 12:7), Jesus twice quoted Hosea 6:6.

19. What kind of punishment does Hosea expect for Israel, according to 9:3, 6; 10:10, 14; 11:5?

20. According to 6:1-3, does Hosea think of punishment as merely punitive or as disciplinary?

21. In 2:14-15, Hosea speaks of the valley of Achor, near the northwestern part of the Dead Sea, close to the route by which the Israelites first entered Canaan in the time of Joshua. What do you think he is saying in this passage?

22. What conditions does Hosea look forward to in 2:16-20? What areas of life will be affected? How does his view of the future in 2:21-23 correspond to 1:2-9?

23. The idea of "holiness" originally denoted the separation between God and men (cf. I Sam. 6:19-20; II Sam. 6:6-7). How does Hosea redefine this idea in 11:8-9?

24. What ideas does Hosea associate with the imagery of "dew" in 6:4; 13:3; 14:5? How would you compare these ideas with the Deuteronomic interpretation of history?

25. What are some of the things you think Hosea might say if he were addressing our society today?

20. Isaiah of Jerusalem (First Isaiah)

The first major prophet in the southern kingdom (Judah), Isaiah was active for about half a century, beginning in 742 B.C. A man of the city, familiar with the temple and the royal court, he sought to advise both king and people during the decades when Judah was increasingly threatened by the expansion of Assyria. He is sometimes known as First Isaiah to distinguish him from other prophets whose writings were later included in the book of Isaiah.

1. Is. 6 describes Isaiah's call to be a prophet. Where did this occur? Do you think there is any connection between "King" in vs. 1 and "King" in vs. 5? How did Isaiah react to his sense of the holiness and glory of Yahweh? What happened? Do you think the ideas in vss. 9-10 indicate the purpose or the consequences of Isaiah's ministry?

2. Is. 1-5 contains sayings from Isaiah's early ministry, in the years after 742 B.C. What does Isaiah think of the people of his time, according to 1:2-6; 2:6-22? Why?

3. What does Isaiah think of the people's worship, according to 1:11-17? Why?

4. What criticisms of conditions in society does Isaiah make in 1:21-23; 3:13-15; 5:8-12, 22-23?

5. What does Isaiah want people to do, according to 1:16-17?

6. In the light of questions 3 to 5, what prophet does Isaiah especially remind you of? Do they have similar backgrounds?

7. Does Isaiah think the people can be forgiven, according to 1:18-20? Does he indicate whether he thinks this is probable?

8. What titles for God does Isaiah use in 1:4, 9, 24; 2:12; 3:1, 15; 5:9, 16, 19, 24?

9. In the "Song of the Vineyard," 5:1-7, Isaiah apparently takes a popular song of the day and

develops it into a parable about Yahweh and Israel. What did Yahweh expect from Israel? What did he find? Note the play on words in vs. 7: justice (mishpat), bloodshed (mispach); righteousness (tsedaqah), cry for help (tse'aqah). For the imagery of bearing fruit, cf. Matt. 7:16-20; John 15:1-11.

10. Much of the material in Is. 7-10 reflects the Syro-Israelite crisis of 733-732 B.C. Assyria was expanding southward along the Mediterranean coast; Syria and Israel formed a coalition to defend themselves; they also attacked Judah to replace king Ahaz by an anti-Assyrian puppet king. Ahaz, weak and vacillating, did not know what to do. What advice did Isaiah give him, according to 7:1-9? Note the play on words in vs. 9: believe (ta'aminu), be established (te'amenu).

11. The Immanuel passage, 7:10-17, also reflects the Syro-Israelite crisis. How old do you think the child must be before he knows the difference between right and wrong (vs. 16)? Before this happens, what relief will come to Judah? What disaster will follow?

12. Several interpretations of Immanuel ("God is with us") are possible: a) Isaiah referred to the boy's childhood as a way of measuring time; b) Isaiah was thinking of the next king, Hezekiah (715-687 B.C.), who was a strong, devout leader; c) Isaiah was predicting the birth of Jesus some seven centuries later (cf. Matt. 1:23). Which interpretation or interpretations do you agree with? Why?

13. The account in II Kings 16 tells how Ahaz reacted at the time of the Syro-Israelite crisis. Did he take Isaiah's advice? What did he do? Why do you think he had an Assyrian altar installed in Jerusalem?

14. Who is speaking in each section of Is. 10:5-19? Note that the speakers change several times. Why does Yahweh allow Assyria to threaten his own people? What is the attitude of the king of Assyria? What will Yahweh do to Assyria?

15. What are some of the characteristics of the ideal king, according to the poems in 9:2-7; 11:1-9?

It is possible that Isaiah originally composed these poems in honor of Hezekiah.

16. In 705 B.C., Judah joined Egypt in revolting against Assyria. What advice did Isaiah give at this time, according to 30:1-5, 15-17; 31:1-3?

17. In 701 B.C. the Assyrian king, Sennacherib, invaded Judah and threatened Jerusalem. What advice did Isaiah give then, according to 31:4-15? What tradition does his advice reflect?

18. How would you summarize the important ideas that Isaiah expressed in his ministry?

21. Micah

A contemporary of Isaiah, Micah was active about 735-700 B.C. He addressed his message to the northern kingdom (which fell to the Assyrians in 721 B.C.) and to the southern kingdom (which was invaded by the Assyrians, but not actually subjugated, in 701 B.C.). Micah lived in the town of Moresheth, about twenty miles southwest of Jerusalem. (Reading: Micah.)

1. In 1:2-9, Micah describes how Yahweh comes out of his temple (perhaps the heavenly counterpart to the earthly temple) to render judgment on Israel and Judah. Why does Yahweh judge them?

2. What conditions in society does Micah criticize in 2:2; 6:11-12; 7:2-6? Of what other prophet do these criticisms remind you?

3. What does Micah think of the "professional" prophets of the day, according to 3:5-7? How does he judge the people's expectations of the prophets, in 2:11?

4. What does Micah think of the political and religious leaders of the time, according to 3:9-11? In our lives as individuals or as a nation, how do you think we can know that "God is on our side" (cf. 3:11)?

5. What does Micah say about his own work and his own feelings, in 3:8; 7:1, 7?

6. What does Micah, as a rural person, think of large cities, according to 1:5; 6:9-16?

7. What does Micah expect to happen to Samaria (i.e., the northern kingdom), according to 1:6? What does he expect to happen to Jerusalem (i.e., the southern kingdom), according to 3:12? How do Micah's expectations for Jerusalem differ from those of Isaiah, according to Is. 31:4-5?

8. What hope for the future does Micah express in 5:2-4? Who had originally come from Bethlehem (cf. I Sam. 17:12)?

9. Review Topic 19, question 8, concerning Hosea's use of the lawsuit imagery. Micah also uses this imagery in 6:1-8. Identify the following sections: summons, charge to witnesses, plaintiff's case, defendant's response, final admonition. Vs. 8 is sometimes regarded as a summary of the preaching of Amos, Hosea, and Isaiah; can you explain this?

10. The "floating oracle" in Mic. 4:1-4 also occurs in Is. 2:2-4. One prophet may have borrowed from the other; or later editors, using a common tradition, may have inserted both passages. What events and conditions does this oracle depict?

22.   The Reform of Josiah

Josiah came to the throne of Judah in 640 B.C., when he was eight years old, and reigned until 609 B.C. Although he may have begun his religious reform in 629 B.C., he carried it out vigorously in 621 B.C. after a forgotten document was discovered in the temple. His reign must be seen in contrast with that of his grandfather, Manasseh (687-642 B.C.). (Reading: II Kings 21-23).

1. According to II Kings 21, what types of foreign worship did Manasseh reintroduce to Judah? What else did he do that the historian condemns? Did the

people of Judah also join in idolatrous worship?

2. What do you think is meant by "the measuring line of Samaria" in II Kings 21:13?

3. What does the historian think of Josiah as a king, according to II Kings 22:2; 23:25?

4. What did Hilkiah the high priest find in the temple, according to II Kings 22:8? Why do you think he found it at this particular time?

5. What did Josiah do when the document was read to him, according to II Kings 22:11-13?

6. Does the reply of Huldah the prophetess give any hint of the contents of the writing, according to II Kings 22:16-17?

7. What is the document called in II Kings 23:2? Does the description of the covenant ceremony in 23:3 give any hint of the contents of the document? Who was involved in this covenant? In what way does it resemble the Sinai covenant? In what way does it resemble the Davidic covenant?

8. Summarize Josiah's religious reform, according to II Kings 23:4-25, as it affected Jerusalem, the cities of Judah, and Samaria. What do you think was the purpose of these measures? What do 23:21, 24 suggest about the contents of the document found in the temple?

9. Did Josiah have any jurisdiction in Samaria? Do you think there was a political aspect to his reform movement?

10. What do you think are the essential characteristics of any genuine religious reform? To what extent do you find these in Josiah's reform?

23. Deuteronomy (D)

The D document in the Pentateuch is represented almost entirely by the book of Deuteronomy. The core of the book (perhaps chs. 5-26; 28) may have been written about 650 B.C. According to one theory, this was the "book of the law" discovered in the temple during the reign of Josiah. The book of Deuteronomy is cast in the form of an address by Moses on Mount Nebo, just before the Israelites crossed the Jordan and entered Canaan.

1. What characteristics of God are expressed in Deut. 4? On the basis of your study so far, would you say that these characteristics, all together, are representative of Old Testament thought?

2. Why do you think the Ten Commandments are given a second time, in Deut. 5? (The word Deuteronomy means "the second law," i.e., the second giving of the law.)

3. Deut. 6:4 is known as the Shema (i.e., "hear," the first word in Hebrew). Later the Shema was extended to include Deut. 6:5-9; 11:13-21; Num. 15:37-41. How did Jesus refer to this, according to Mark 12:28-34?

4. How would you describe the Israelite understanding of "religious education," according to Deut. 6:20-25?

5. What should the Israelites do when they enter Canaan, according to Deut. 7:1-5? **Why?**

6. Why did God choose Israel and give them the land of Canaan, according to Deut. 7:6-11; 9:4-6?

7. What danger may arise from national prosperity, according to Deut. 8:6-20? Do you think this danger affects other nations as well?

8. Why do you think that Deut. 12:1-14 requires that worship be centralized in one place? How would you compare this passage with Josiah's actions in II Kings 23?

9. How were Hebrew slaves to be treated, according to

Deut. 15:12-18?

10. What were the three annual religious festivals, according to Deut. 16:1-17? Cf. II kings 23:21-23.

11. What restrictions are to be placed on the king, according to Deut. 17:14-20? Why do you think the idea of kingship itself is not questioned here? Do you think similar restrictions would be applicable to the president of the United States?

12. What "social security" type of provision was made for the sojourner, the fatherless, and the widow, according to Deut. 24:19-22?

24. Jeremiah

Jeremiah, who was active about 626-587 B.C., lived during a time of rapid change when Judah was caught up in the maelstrom of world events. Assyria fell in 612 B.C.; Egypt made a brief, unsuccessful attempt to fill the power vacuum; the Babylonians under Nebuchadnezzar defeated Egypt in 605 B.C. and established themselves as heirs of the Assyrian empire. In 597 B.C., Nebuchadnezzar plundered the Jerusalem temple and carried some of the Jewish people into exile. In 587 B.C., punishing the Jews for revolting, he burned the temple, demolished the city walls, and took more Jews into exile. Jeremiah sought to interpret the meaning of these events and at the same time look beyond them to a better day to come.

1. Jeremiah's call to be a prophet is recorded in 1:4-10. How did he react to his call? How did Yahweh reassure him? Note the verbs in vs. 10. Was Jeremiah's work to be critical, constructive, or both?

2. The vision or parable of the almond branch, 1:11-12, uses a play on words between "almond" (shaqed) and "watching" (shoqed). What do you think it means to say that God is watching over his word?

3. The vision or parable of the boiling pot, 1:13-19, was probably understood, at least later in

Jeremiah's career, to refer to the threat from Babylon. According to this vision, what will Yahweh do? What instrument will he use? Why will he take this action? What does he promise Jeremiah?

4. Examples of Jeremiah's early preaching are contained in 2:1-4:4. How does Jeremiah assess the wilderness period (2:2)? What traditions does he refer to in 2:4-8? Why? When did Israel's apostasy begin (2:7)? What does he think of religious and political leaders (2:8)? On the basis of these questions, what earlier prophet do you think influenced Jeremiah at this point?

5. In 11:1-17, Jeremiah speaks of "this covenant" (probably the Sinai covenant; possibly also a reference to the Deuteronomic reform of 621 B.C., seen as a renewal of the Sinai covenant). Which one of the Ten Commandments does he stress? Does he think the people have kept this commandment? What does he say Yahweh will do?

6. If Jeremiah supported the Deuteronomic reform initially, he apparently came to believe that it was not bringing about a genuine change in the people's religious attitudes. What criticisms of the people does he make in 6:16; 8:8-9, 18-21; 9:4-11?

7. When Josiah (640-609 B.C.) was followed by his son Jehoiakim (609-598 B.C.), Jeremiah saw a great difference between them. What does he say about them in 22:13-19?

8. In 609 B.C., Jeremiah delivered a sermon at the temple in Jerusalem. The sermon is in ch. 7, and the reaction to it is described in ch. 26. What themes did Jeremiah develop in the sermon? How did the listeners react? What saved Jeremiah's life on this occasion?

9. According to ch. 36, what did Jeremiah dictate to Baruch? What did Jehoiakim do when the scroll was read to him? What did Jeremiah do then?

10. After 605 B.C., Babylon became a threat to Judah. What reason does Jeremiah give for this threat, according to 4:11-18? How does Jeremiah himself feel, according to 4:19-22?

11. In 4:23-28, Jeremiah depicts a scene in which the
earth returns to its state of pre-creation chaos
("waste and void," vs. 23; the same phrase as in
Gen. 1:2). What do you think he wishes to signify
by this imagery?

12. What does Jeremiah think of other prophets, who
ignore or minimize the threat from Babylon,
according to 5:30-31; 6:13-15; 14:11-16; 23:16-22?

13. In 18:1-12, Jeremiah compares Yahweh to a potter
and Israel to a piece of clay. Does Jeremiah use
this imagery to signify that the people have
freedom of choice and action, or the opposite?
Explain your answer. How would you relate
Jeremiah's thought here to the threat from Babylon?

14. How does Jeremiah interpret the threat from
Babylon in 25:1-14? What have the people done
wrong? In what sense can Nebuchadnezzar, the king
of Babylon, be described as the "servant" of
Yahweh (25:9; cf. 27:6; 43:10)? What will happen
later to Babylon? Why? (Note that the Babylonian
empire came to power in 605 B.C. and fell in 539
B.C.)

15. In a number of passages Jeremiah expresses his own
feelings of loneliness, discouragement, and doubt:
4:19-22; 8:18-9:3; 11:18-23; 12:1-6; 15:15-21;
17:14-18; 18:18-23; 20:7-12, 14-18. Does he want
Judah to be threatened by Babylon, in 4:19-22?
Why does he feel "wounded" in 8:18-9:3? Why does
he compare God to a "deceitful brook" in 15:15-21?
How does God reassure him? What has Jeremiah tried
to do for the people, according to 18:18-23? How
have the people reacted?

16. When Zedekiah (597-587 B.C.) came to the throne,
Jeremiah at first thought that he might listen to
his preaching. What hopes for the reign of
Zedekiah did he have, according to 23:1-8? (The
words "The Lord is our righteousness" in vs. 6 are
a play on the name Zedekiah.)

17. What advice did Jeremiah give Zedekiah, in chs.
27-28? Why did he wear a yoke? What did he do
when Hananiah broke the yoke?

18. After Nebuchadnezzar took some of the people into

exile in 597 B.C., Jeremiah saw a vision of "good figs" and "bad figs" (ch. 24). What does each represent? Does the chapter indicate whether Zedekiah was receptive to Jeremiah's advice?

19. In 29:1-14, a letter from Jeremiah to the exiles of 597 B.C. has been preserved. What advice does Jeremiah give to these exiles?

20. According to 32:1-44, Jeremiah bought a field at Anathoth, several miles northeast of Jerusalem, at the very time the Babylonian army was besieging Jerusalem. Was this a good time to buy real estate? Why do you think Jeremiah bought the field? What hopes for the future does he express in 32:36-44?

21. In 31:31-34, Jeremiah looks forward to a "new covenant" from Yahweh. In what ways will it be like the Sinai covenant? In what way will it be different?

22. Why will Yahweh restore Israel, according to 31:1-6?

23. Some people in the time of Jesus compared him to Jeremiah (Matt. 16:14). Why do you think they did this?

25. Habakkuk

The prophet Habakkuk was apparently active during the closing years of the seventh century, when Judah was under Assyrian rule (until 612 B.C.) and then under Babylonian domination (after 605 B.C.). In his dialogue with Yahweh he raises the question of theodicy - i.e., how God can be considered just when there is so much evil in the world. (Reading: Habakkuk.)

1. Habakkuk's first complaint is in 1:2-4. What kinds of injustice are the people of Judah suffering?

2. In 1:2-4, Habakkuk may be describing the oppression that the people are subjected to under Assyrian rule. He may also be describing conditions under

their own king, Jehoiakim (609-598 B.C.). What did Jeremiah think of Jehoiakim (cf. Jer. 22:13-19)? Do you think Habakkuk could be referring to both the Assyrians and Jehoiakim?

3. Yahweh answers Habakkuk in 1:5-11. Why is Yahweh bringing the Chaldeans (Babylonians) against Judah? What kind of men are the Chaldeans? Explain, in particular, the meaning of 1:7b and 1:11b.

4. Habakkuk's second complaint is in 1:12-2:1. How does he think of Yahweh? Why does he regard Babylon as a new problem, rather than a solution to the injustice that Judah is suffering?

5. Can you think of several modern examples of the problem that Habakkuk refers to in 1:13?

6. Yahweh answers Habakkuk in 2:2-5. Does Yahweh promise an immediate solution to the problem of evil and injustice? What should the righteous person do in the meantime? Note that 2:4b is apparently explained further by 3:16b.

7. In 2:6-20, Habakkuk criticizes those who oppress others or practice idolatry. Do you think he could be referring to the Assyrians, Jehoiakim, the Babylonians, or some combination of these?

8. The "prayer" of Habakkuk in ch. 3 is primarily a theophanic psalm, giving a vivid description of God's intervention in history. It may be the "vision" mentioned in 2:2. What major event of the past does Habakkuk refer to in 3:8? Why?

9. Some writers in the Old Testament thought of material prosperity as a sign of the presence and blessing of God (e.g., Deut. 7:12-15). What attitude does Habakkuk have, according to 3:17-19?

26. Ezekiel

One of the exiles carried to Babylon in the deportation of 597 B.C., Ezekiel was active about 593-571 B.C. His career, therefore, spanned the fall of Jerusalem in 587 B.C. Like Jeremiah, he sought to interpret the meaning of this event and then look beyond it to a new beginning.

1. Ezekiel's vision of the majestic glory of Yahweh, 1:4-28, draws its imagery from the cherubim (mythical creatures, part animal and part human) that guarded the ark in the Jerusalem temple, and perhaps also from early tradition concerning Yahweh's revelation at Sinai (cf. Ex. 24:10). What do you think this vision suggests about the nature of God? What place had the glory of Yahweh come from, according to 10:18-22? Where will it eventually return, according to 43:1-5?

2. What commission does Yahweh give to Ezekiel at this time, according to 2:1-3:3? What do you think it means that Yahweh tells him to eat a scroll?

3. What criticisms does Ezekiel make of the people of Judah, according to 6:11-14; 22:23-31? Does Ezekiel, a priest, limit his criticisms to ritual matters?

4. Describe the signs, or representative actions, that Ezekiel is to perform, according to 4:1-17; 12:1-11; 24:15-24. What do they mean?

5. What other nation does Ezekiel suggest Yahweh will use as an instrument to punish his own people, according to 7:23-27? Did Jeremiah say the same?

6. What expectations does Ezekiel have for the group of exiles in Babylon, according to 11:14-21? Did Jeremiah have the same expectations?

7. What proverb were the people repeating, according to 18:1-4? How did they apply it to their own situation? How did Ezekiel react to it? Cf. Jer. 31:29-30 and Deut. 24:16.

8. For the early view of corporate responsibility, cf. Topic 11, question 7. For an early view of individual responsibility within the context of the community, cf. Topic 10, question 8. Was Ezekiel's emphasis on individual responsibility an entirely new idea? Did he think of the individual person in isolation from the community or as standing within the community?

9. Does Ezekiel believe that Yahweh is ready to forgive the wicked person who repents, according to 33:10-20? Why do you think Ezekiel raised this issue?

10. What news did Ezekiel receive, in 33:21? Note how his message changes in the following chapters.

11. In what three ways does Ezekiel use the word "shepherd" in 34:1-31? What will Yahweh do as shepherd? Do you think it is significant that Ezekiel looks forward to a new Davidic ruler as "prince" (34:24)? Cf. I Sam. 10:1, and also Ezek. 37:24.

12. According to 36:22-32, does Israel deserve to be restored to her land? Why will Yahweh do this? Compare 36:26-28 with Jer. 31:31-34.

13. Who are the "dry bones" in 37:1-14? What does Ezekiel mean when he says that the bones will be brought back to life?

14. What do the two sticks represent in 37:15-28?

15. At the end of his book Ezekiel depicts a new temple that is to be built in Jerusalem. What group of priests will alone have the privilege of offering sacrifice (40:46)? What other functions will they have (44:23-24)? What warnings does Ezekiel give about political leaders (45:8-9; 46:18)?

27. The P Document

According to the documentary theory of the Pentateuch, the P (priestly) document was written about 550 B.C., during the time of the exile. The author (or circle of writers) sought to preserve priestly traditions from the Jerusalem temple and delineate the role of Israel in relation to God's purposes for all mankind. Later, about 400 B.C., the P document served as the literary basis for the composition of the entire Pentateuch (JEDP).

1. It is uncertain whether the P document originated

among those who remained in Judah or those who were taken to Babylon as exiles. How did the people in Judah feel, according to Lamentations 5:1-22? How did the exiles in Babylon feel, according to Psalm 137:1-9?

2. As a survey of the four main sections of the P document, read Gen. 1:1-2:4b (creation of the world), Gen. 9:1-17 (covenant with Noah), Gen. 17: 1-8 (covenant with Abraham), Ex. 19:1-2a; 24:15-18 (revelation at Mt. Sinai). How broad is the scope of each section? What name is used for God in each section? Do you find any correlation between the scope of a section and the name used for God?

3. For characteristics of the P account of creation, review Topic 3, questions 1-8. What is the theme of Psalm 8? How would you compare it to the P account of creation?

4. What were the dimensions of Noah's ark, according to Gen. 6:9-22? In an ancient Sumerian flood story, a man named Utnapishtim built a boat measuring 120x120x120 cubits.

5. Compare the P view of the world (Gen. 1:6-10) with the P account of the flood (Gen. 7:11, 18-21, 24). What is the relation between them - i.e., what almost happens in the flood?

6. To whom does the covenant with Noah (Gen. 9:1-17) apply? What ethical commandment does God give at this time? Is man still made in the image of God, even after the flood? What do you think this means? What promise does God make in this covenant? What is the sign of the covenant?

7. To whom does the covenant with Abraham (Gen. 17:1-8) apply? What promises does God make in this covenant? Did the promise in Gen. 17:8 come true in Abraham's own time? In light of this, what significance attaches to the accounts concerning the cave of Machpelah (Gen. 23:1-20; 25:7-10)?

8. What special name is revealed to Moses, according to Ex. 6:2-9? How does this passage link the Mosaic period with the earlier patriarchal period?

9. The P document gives no independent account of the

making of the Sinai covenant (although it describes the sabbath as a "perpetual covenant," Gen. 31:16). It views the sojourn at Sinai as the occasion when God revealed regulations of a priestly and ritual nature. Why do you think these matters were important to the writer, during the exile?

10. What was the ark to look like, according to Ex. 25: 10-22? What was the mercy seat? What was its function?

11. What will Yahweh do, according to Ex. 29:43-46? Why were these promises especially meaningful during the time of the exile?

12. What is the purpose of sacrifice, according to Lev. 5:17-19? According to Lev. 6:1-7? Is sacrifice a way of appeasing God or a means that God himself has provided for extending forgiveness?

13. What animals were the Israelites permitted to eat, according to Lev. 11:1-8? Why do Jews today refrain from eating pork?

14. Describe the ethical concerns that are reflected in Lev. 19:1-18. How would you compare them to the Ten Commandments (Ex. 20:2-17, perhaps from the E document)? Do you think these ethical concerns are incompatible with the priestly interests of the P document? Explain.

15. Review the four major sections of the P document (question 2). What meaning would the ideas in each section have to a writer living in the middle of the sixth century B.C., when Judah had lost its independence, the temple had been destroyed, and many of the people had been taken into exile in Babylon? Explain.

28. Second Isaiah

Chapters 40-55 in the book of Isaiah are often attributed to an anonymous prophet, known as Second Isaiah, who was active about 540 B.C. among the exiles in Babylon. In joyous, lyrical poetry he proclaimed that Yahweh would soon lead the exiles home, just as he had originally freed the Israelites from bondage in Egypt and brought them into their homeland. (Reading: Isaiah 40-55.)

1. What foreign power threatened Judah in the time of I Isaiah (cf. Is. 7:17; 8:5-8; 10:12)? Was the Jerusalem temple standing (cf. Is. 6:1)? What foreign power rules over the Jews in the time of II Isaiah (cf. Is. 43:14; 47:1)? What ruler is about to take over and establish his own empire (cf. Is. 45:1; 48:14)? In what condition are Jerusalem and the temple (cf. Is. 44:26, 28; 52:2)?

2. What reason does II Isaiah give for the destruction of Jerusalem in 587 B.C., according to 42:24-25? ("Jacob" is a poetic synonym for "Israel," i.e., the covenant people of Yahweh.) Would Jeremiah and Ezekiel agree with this explanation?

3. How do the exiles in Babylon feel, according to 40:27-31; 49:14?

4. What message does II Isaiah bring to the exiles, in 40:1-2, 28-31; 43:3-7; 44;21-23; 49:13; 51:11; 54:7-8? In light of these passages, what do you think is meant by the "good tidings" of 40:9; 41:27; 52:7? What mood does II Isaiah feel is appropriate, according to 42:10-13; 44:23; 49:13?

5. How is Yahweh making use of Cyrus, according to 41:2-4, 25; 44;28-45:8; 45:13; 46;11; 48:14-16? Notice that Cyrus is described as Yahweh's "anointed one" (messiah) in 45:1. Did this term have a single, exclusive meaning at this time? Can you think of examples from other prophets in which Yahweh used a non-Israelite ruler or nation to accomplish his purposes?

6. In his own account, in the Cyrus cylinder, Cyrus attributed his success to the Babylonian god Marduk. II Isaiah believed that it was Yahweh who was guiding Cyrus' career. Who do you think was "right"? Explain.

7. What belief about Yahweh does II Isaiah remind the exiles of, as a way of reassuring them that Yahweh can and will deliver them? Cf. 40:27-31; 45:18-19; 51:12-16. Was this belief also important to the

writer of the P document?

8. How does II Isaiah's language reflect the terminology of the Babylonian creation myth in 51:9b–10a? Cf. Gen. 1:2; Job 9:8; Pss. 74:13–14; 89:9–10.

9. How does II Isaiah "up-date" the theme of the promise to Noah, in 54:9–10? Cf. Gen. 9:1–17.

10. Why do you think II Isaiah refers to Abraham, in 41:8–10; 51:1–3? Did the writer of the P document find a similar significance in the covenant with Abraham?

11. What important event in Israel's early history does II Isaiah refer to in 43:16–17; 51:10b; 52:11–12; 55:12–13? What parallels does he find between this event and the action that Yahweh is about to take? Did I Isaiah emphasize this event (or tradition) in his own preaching?

12. What tradition, closely related to the one above, does II Isaiah refer to in 40:3; 41:17–20; 43:19–21; 48:21?

13. Although II Isaiah does not mention the Sinai covenant, he may believe that its provisions will still apply in the future as a guide for Israel and even for other peoples. Do you find any allusions to the Sinai covenant in 40:18–20; 42:4; 43:10–11; 45:5; 48:17; 51:4–8?

14. Unlike Ezekiel, II Isaiah makes no mention of the restoration of a Davidic ruler. Instead he seems to "democratize" the tradition of the Davidic covenant in 55:1–5. Can you explain what this means?

15. What is Yahweh's ultimate purpose, according to 42:5–9; 45:22; 49:6, 8? What is Israel's role in carrying out Yahweh's purpose?

16. Compare Is. 43:11; 44:6; 45:5, 22 with Deut. 4:35, 39; Ex. 20:3. Do these passages all have the same view of God? How would you explain the difference?

17. In 44:9–20, II Isaiah describes a visit to a workshop that makes idols for use in the Babylonian religion. What is the essence of idolatry,

according to this passage? Cf. especially vss.
16-17.

18. II Isaiah uses a number of titles for Yahweh to
    bring out his understanding of Yahweh's nature and
    actions. These include, e.g., Holy One (of Israel),
    Savior, Redeemer. What other titles can you find?

19. A special way in which II Isaiah refers to Yahweh
    is the solemn self-predication "I am He." In the
    Old Testament this phrase occurs almost exclusively
    in II Isaiah. What ideas does II Isaiah associate
    with this phrase, in 43:10, 13, 25; 48:12; 51:12?

20. The word tsedaqah is translated as "righteousness"
    or "deliverance" in II Isaiah. What term does II
    Isaiah use in poetic parallelism with this word in
    45:8; 51:5, 6, 8? In light of this, what do you
    think is the meaning of God's "righteousness" for
    II Isaiah? Cf. Ps. 24:5.

21. Who is the "servant" of Yahweh, according to 41:8-
    10; 44:1-5, 21-22; 45:4? What does Yahweh do for
    the servant, in each passage?

22. Four passages in II Isaiah are sometimes designated
    the "servant poems": 42:1-4; 49:1-6; 50:4-9; 52:13-
    53:12. Interpreters differ on the question whether
    the servant should be understood as a group (the
    people of Israel) or a single person (of the past,
    the present, or the future). Some interpret the
    poems in terms of the concept of corporate person-
    ality, in which the individual represents the group
    and the reality of the group can be expressed in the
    individual person. What is the task or function of
    the servant, in each of these passages?

23. In the second servant poem, the servant is identi-
    fied as Israel (49:3) but then is given a task that
    affects Israel (49:5). Can you think of an
    explanation for this?

24. The fourth servant poem apparently has three main
    parts: an introductory announcement by Yahweh
    (52:13-15); a confessional lament by the nations
    of the world, represented by their kings (53:1-9);
    a concluding summary by Yahweh, referring to the
    ultimate vindication of the servant (53:10-12).
    According to this analysis, what is the scope of the

50

servant's work? What verses express the concept of vicarious suffering (i.e., the suffering of the innocent on behalf of others)?

25. The opening passage in II Isaiah utilizes the imagery of the heavenly council, in which Yahweh sits in heaven and addresses his heavenly attendants or messengers (40:1-11). For the concept of the heavenly council, cf. I Kings 22:19; Jer. 23:18, 22; Ps. 89:5-7. Yahweh speaks to his attendants in 40:1-2 (the imperatives are plural); an attendant speaks in 40:3-5; another attendant speaks in 40:6a, 8-11; II Isaiah speaks in 40:6b-7, reflecting at this point the discouragement of the exiles. By using this imagery II Isaiah suggests that his opportunity to hear the decisions announced in the heavenly council constituted his call to be a prophet. What task does he receive? How would you compare this passage with the call of I Isaiah (Is. 6)?

26. The salvation oracle is a distinctive type of speech that II Isaiah uses a number of times (41: 8-13, 14-16; 43:1-4, 5-7; 44:1-5). This pattern apparently originated in the Jerusalem temple, when a priest assured a worshiper, discouraged by some misfortune, that Yahweh had heard his prayer and would help him. II Isaiah utilizes this form of speech to reassure a despairing people that Yahweh will restore them from exile. The first salvation oracle illustrates the typical structure (41:8-13): address ("But you, Israel, my servant..."); phrase of reassurance ("fear not"); supporting clauses, in past or present ("for I am with you... I have strengthened you..."); message of deliverance ("those who war against you shall be as nothing..."); self-predication of Yahweh ("For I, Yahweh, your God..."). Can you identify this structure in the other salvation oracles? Why do you think II Isaiah used this pattern of speech?

27. Pre-exilic prophets sometimes used the imagery of the trial scene, in which Yahweh appeared as the prosecuting attorney and accused Israel of not fulfilling her obligations under the Sinai covenant (cf. Hos. 4:1-3; Mic. 6:1-8). II Isaiah uses this imagery in 43:25-28 to show that Yahweh had been justified in allowing Jerusalem to be destroyed in 587 B.C. The further consequence of the trial,

however, appears in 44:1-5. What type of passage is this? Does it follow "logically" from the trial scene? If not, how would you explain the fact that II Isaiah links it closely with the trial scene?

28. II Isaiah alludes to the imagery of the trial scene again in 51:21-23, but he employs it in a different way. What role does Yahweh have here? How does this role fit in with II Isaiah's message? For a similar use of this imagery, cf. Ps. 74:22; Jer. 50:34; 51:36.

29. In 41:1-16 and 41:21-29, II Isaiah employs a different type of trial scene, in which the purpose is not to assign responsibility for wrongdoing but to adjudicate between competing claims. In these scenes Yahweh brings into court the other peoples of the world, together with their gods, to determine who actually controls the course of history. How does Yahweh state his case, in 41:2-4? What is the effect on the other nations, in 41:5-7? What is the result for Israel, in 41:8-16? What pattern of speech does II Isaiah use to state this result?

30. In 46:1-4, II Isaiah depicts the flight of the Babylonians, as they flee from their city and take with them statues of their gods Bel (Marduk) and Nebo (son of Marduk). How does he contrast these gods with Yahweh?

31. II Isaiah belonged to a small country that had suffered military defeat, loss of political independence, and exile. The United States, in contrast, is one of the "superpowers" of the modern world. Given these differences, what themes in II Isaiah's message do you think are still applicable today?

29. Restoration and Reform

For two centuries after Cyrus conquered Babylon (539 B.C.), the Jews lived under Persian rule. Although they enjoyed some measure of self-government, they faced the tasks of economic recovery and spiritual renewal. Participation in the worship of the temple and obedience to the Law increasingly became hallmarks of Judaism

during this period. (Reading: Haggai 1-2; Zechariah
1-8; Nehemiah and Ezra as indicated.)

1. In 538 B.C., Cyrus of Persia issued a decree concerning the Jews. The decree is preserved in two
   forms, in Ezra 1:2-4 and 6:3-5. Together, what do
   these passages indicate that Cyrus did for the Jews?
   How does the decree suggest that Persian policy
   toward conquered peoples was different from previous
   Babylonian and Assyrian policies?

2. Shortly after the decree of Cyrus, some of the
   Jewish exiles in Babylon returned to Judah. Under
   the leadership of Jeshua (or Joshua, the high
   priest) and Zerubbabel (the civil leader), they took
   steps to restore proper forms of worship. What did
   they do, according to the account in Ezra 3:1-13?
   What did the Samaritans want to do, according to
   Ezra 4:1-5? What happened after Zerubbabel refused
   their request?

3. The prophet Haggai began his work in 520 B.C. What
   economic conditions does he describe, according to
   Haggai 1:2-11? What explanation for them does he
   give? What does he want the people to do? Did the
   people do this, according to Haggai 1:12-15?

4. The idea of "shaking," in Haggai 2:6-9, 21-22, may
   echo the fact that nationalistic uprisings occurred
   throughout the Persian empire when Darius (522-486
   B.C.) came to the throne. How does Haggai interpret
   the significance of this situation for the Jews?

5. Note that Haggai refers to two leaders - one
   religious (Joshua, the high priest) and one civil
   (Zerubbabel, the governor, apparently the grandson
   of Jehoiachin, one of the last kings of Judah).
   Does he usually mention them together? Which one
   does he mention first?

6. What special promise does Yahweh make to Zerubbabel,
   according to Haggai 2:20-23? For the "signet ring,"
   as a sign that the king acts on behalf of Yahweh,
   cf. Jer. 22:24.

7. The prophet Zechariah also began his work in 520
   B.C., about two months after Haggai. What does
   Zechariah think of the preaching of the pre-exilic

prophets, according to Zech. 1:2-6; 7:1-14? Does he think that ritual observance without ethical righteousness is acceptable to Yahweh?

8. Zechariah often spoke in the form of "visions," although the meaning of details is sometimes obscure. How would you explain the meaning of the first, third, and sixth visions, in Zech. 1:7-17; 2:1-13; 5:1-4?

9. What does Yahweh commission Joshua to do, according to Zech. 3:1-10?

10. The phrase "my servant the Branch" in Zech. 3:8 is a reference to the civil governor, Zerubbabel. For "Branch" as a designation of the Davidic king, cf. Is. 11:1; Jer. 23:5. What hope do you think Zechariah is expressing at this point? Cf. also Zech. 4:6-10.

11. In Zech. 6:9-15, note that Joshua is designated as the Branch. Some interpreters believe that the promise originally referred to Zerubbabel, rather than Joshua. Zerubbabel dropped out of sight after 515 B.C., without restoring the Davidic kingdom, and the Persian rulers apparently did not continue to appoint governors of Judah who belonged to the Davidic line. Later editors apparently transferred the promise to Joshua, as a way of indicating that the high priest would be civil as well as religious leader of the Jewish community.

12. Nehemiah came to Judah as governor in 445 B.C. According to Neh. 1:1-2:20, where was he living? What did he do? Why did he want to go to Judah?

13. According to Neh. 4:1-23; 6:15-19, Nehemiah encouraged the Jews to rebuild the wall around Jerusalem. Why do you think Sanballat (governor of Samaria) opposed rebuilding the wall? How did the Jews protect themselves? How long did it take to rebuild the wall?

14. What religious reforms did Nehemiah undertake, according to Neh. 13:15-27? Why do you think he did this?

15. Ezra probably came to Judah in 428 B.C. (the date is uncertain). According to Ezra 7:1-10, where was

Ezra living? How is he described? Why did he want
to go to Judah?

16. According to Neh. 8:1-18, what "book" did Ezra
    bring with him? What did he do with it? What was
    the role of the Levites (Neh. 8:7-9)?

17. Neh. 9:1-38 gives a long prayer by Ezra, followed
    by a ceremony of covenant renewal. What themes
    does Ezra express in this prayer? Why do you think
    the prayer precedes the renewal of the covenant?
    What covenant do you think is being renewed?

18. What measure did Ezra take, according to Ezra 10:9-
    11? Was it more stringent, or less, than Nehemiah's
    action (cf. Neh. 13:23-27)?

19. As you review events during this period, why do you
    think the temple and the Law became so important to
    the Jews?

30. Psalms

Although the book of Psalms received its final
form during the post-exilic period, many of the individual psalms, in all probability, date from pre-exilic
times. The psalms reflect the experience of the
Israelite people as they praised God for his goodness,
recounted his gracious deeds on their behalf, and
sought his help in times of need.

1. The psalms suggest that God makes himself known in
    several ways. How is God revealed, according to
    Ps. 8? Does this thought lead the writer to think
    of man's insignificance or man's special position
    of honor in the world? How is God revealed,
    according to Ps. 135? What conclusion does the
    writer draw about the relation between Yahweh and
    the gods of other nations? How is God revealed,
    according to Ps. 119? What attitudes does the
    writer express about this way of knowing God?

2. The question above illustrates three ways in which
    God makes himself known. Which do you think is
    most representative of the Old Testament as a whole?

Which received special emphasis in the post-exilic period? What significance do you think people attribute to them today?

3. Review Topic 2, concerning the traditions of Israel's faith (patriarchs, Exodus, Sinai, etc.). What traditions can you identify in Pss. 78; 105; 136? Note that these psalms emphasize the idea of God's deeds of deliverance in history. Which psalm connects this idea with the theme of creation? Which psalms regard it as a basis for praise or thanksgiving to God? Which psalm contrasts God's deeds of deliverance with the failure of the people to respond in gratitude and obedience? Which psalm associates God's deeds with his law?

4. The main theme of Ps. 89 is the covenant with David. What promises does God make to David and his descendants? Why do you think the writer refers to God's role as Creator, in vss. 9-12, 36-37? What problem has arisen, according to vss. 38-45?

5. Several psalms deal with occasions in the lives of the Israelite kings: coronation ceremonies (Pss. 2; 110), a royal wedding (Ps. 45), an intercessory prayer on behalf of the king (Ps. 72). What is the source of the king's power, according to Pss. 2 and 110? What does God promise the king in these psalms? Note in Ps. 45:4 that the king has the function of leading in warfare. How is this function qualified? How does the author of Ps. 72 suggest that a good king seeks to promote the welfare of his people?

6. Ps. 84 reflects a pilgrimage to the temple in Jerusalem. How does the writer think of God? How would you explain vs. 7? Ps. 122 is another pilgrim song, probably sung by pilgrims as they are ready to leave Jerusalem and go home. What memories do they take with them?

7. Pss. 15, 24, and 100 refer to persons entering the temple courts to worship. According to Ps. 15, what requirements must a person meet in order to worship? Are they ethical or ritual in nature? Compare these with the requirements in Ps. 24:4. Ps. 24:7-10 may depict a procession in which the ark of Yahweh was carried into the temple (cf. Ps. 132:8-9). Can you identify the speakers in these

verses? What terms or ideas does the author of
Ps. 100 use in describing God?

8. The songs of Zion celebrate Jerusalem as God's city
and the temple as his dwelling-place. How extensive is God's sovereignty, according to Ps. 46?
What are the "works" of Yahweh, according to this
psalm? Of what prophet does vs. 10 remind you?
In Ps. 48:2, how would you explain the words "joy
of all the earth"? Note that Ps. 50 depicts a
theophany of Yahweh on Mt. Zion, utilizing the
imagery of the lawsuit. What is true worship,
according to this psalm?

9. Several psalms celebrate Yahweh's role as king;
e.g., Pss. 47; 93; 96; 97. These psalms may have
been used in a New Year's festival in the Jerusalem
temple in the fall of each year. What is the extent
of Yahweh's kingship, according to Ps. 47? What did
Yahweh do for Israel, according to vss. 3-4? What
will he do for the peoples of the world, according
to vss. 8-9? How would you interpret Ps. 47:8-9 in
the light of Gen. 12:3? Review Topic 1, question 1,
concerning the Babylonian creation myth. Can you
find an echo of this myth in Ps. 93? Of what
prophet does Ps. 96:1-5 remind you? What will
Yahweh do, according to Ps. 96:13? Is this consistent with Ps. 47:8-9?

10. A number of psalms are primarily concerned with the
praise of God. Examples are Pss. 33; 103; 145; 148;
149. Why should God be praised, according to Ps.
33:4-5? What does God see when he "looks down from
heaven," according to Ps. 33:13-19? What does it
mean to "fear" Yahweh, according to Ps. 33:18?
What "benefits" does God give people, according to
Ps. 103:1-5? How does God treat people, according
to Ps. 103:6-14? What view of human nature is
reflected in Ps. 103:15-16? How does the author of
Ps. 145 think of God, especially in vss. 8-9, 14-20?
Do the terms in Ps. 145:11 remind you of any part of
the Lord's Prayer? How would you compare the
attitudes toward foreign countries in Ps. 148 and
Ps. 149?

11. Some psalms reflect a situation in which an individual person expresses trust in God or thanks God
for his help in time of need. What is the main
theme of Ps. 23? How is God depicted in Ps. 23:1-4?

Cf. Ezek. 34:11-16. How is God depicted in Ps. 23: 5-6? What experience did the writer of Ps. 30 have? What does he thank God for? How does he think of the underworld (Sheol, or the Pit)? What does the author of Ps. 32 thank God for? What advice does he give? Does the author of Ps. 138 explain exactly what he is thanking God for? In light of this, do you think the psalm is meaningful for other people to use? How does the writer of Ps. 139:7-12 think of the underworld? How would you compare this with Ps. 30:8-9?

12. Pss. 67 and 124 thank God for some good fortune that affects the life of the people as a whole. What does each thank God for? Note the world-wide outlook of Ps. 67. Of what prophet does this remind you?

13. Many psalms reflect a situation in which an individual person asks for God's help or forgiveness. Why does the author of Ps. 10 think that God has "hidden" himself? How does he describe the wicked? What does he ask God to do? From what situation does the writer of Ps. 22 seek deliverance (cf. especially vss. 14-17)? What do people say that makes his suffering even worse (vss. 6-8)? Is there any indication in the psalm that God hears his prayer? Why is this sometimes called the Passion Psalm (cf. Mark 15:34)? What does the author of Ps. 51 ask for? Against whom has he sinned? Does he regard his punishment as just? What kind of sacrifice does he think is acceptable to God? What does the writer of Ps. 77 think may have happened to God's love and compassion? How does he deal with this problem? Why does the author of Ps. 130 feel alienated from God? How does he hope this sense of alienation will be overcome?

14. In some psalms the community of Israel asks for God's help. What historical event do you think is reflected in Ps. 74? Why do you think a hymn in honor of God (vss. 12-17) is inserted into the lament? Does the hymn express the people's faith or strengthen their faith, or both? What is the theme of Ps. 90? Why is God angry? What do the people ask for?

15. Some psalms present the writers' reflections on the meaning of life. Ps. 1 may reflect the situation

of post-exilic Judaism, when the Jews faced the problem of preserving the identity of their religion. What does the righteous man avoid? What does he do? What reward does he receive? Would you agree that piety always leads to prosperity? Ps. 49 reflects a situation in which a man is being oppressed by wealthy persecutors. What is the general fate of mankind, which he thinks his persecutors will share? What future does he anticipate for himself? Ps. 73 presents a similar situation, in which a man was envious of the prosperity of the wicked. How does he depict the wicked? How does he describe himself? How did he react at first toward God? What does he expect will happen to the wicked? What value does he assign to his relationship with God? Does he expect it to continue beyond the limits of his present life?

31. Proverbs

A collection of sayings illustrating the value of wisdom, the book of Proverbs contrasts the life of the wise, righteous person with that of the foolish and wicked. The present form of the book comes from the post-exilic period, although many of the sayings undoubtedly originated much earlier. (Reading: Proverbs.)

1. Prov. 3:33 has the form of antithetic parallelism, in which a line or verse is contrasted with a following line or verse. Prov. 2:20 illustrates synonymous parallelism, in which a line or verse expresses the same idea as the following line or verse. Prov. 4:4 illustrates ascending parallelism, in which the thought is developed from one line or verse to the next. Sometimes two types are combined, as in 2:21-22 (synonymous parallelism within antithetic parallelism). What kinds of parallelism do you find in 3:13-15; 12:14; 13:21; 15:23?

2. Who can benefit from wisdom, according to 1:2-6? What other words are used, more or less freely, as synonyms of wisdom in this passage?

3. From what source can a person receive wisdom,

according to 1:8; 6:20? How does one acquire
wisdom according to 2:1-5? How does one receive
it according to 2:6-15; 3:5-8? Do you find any
inconsistency among these ways of receiving wisdom?
Explain.

4. Why does wisdom reprove men, according to 1:20-33?

5. Does the practice of wisdom bring rewards, accor-
    ding to 3:1-4, 9-10; 9:11; 13:21; 22:4? Are the
    rewards material or spiritual, or both? Do you
    think that religion is simply a matter of seeking
    rewards? If not, what is the place of rewards?

6. Is there any suggestion that wisdom has value in
    itself, in 3:13-18; 8:10-11?

7. Because the Hebrew word for wisdom (chokmah) is
    feminine, the idea is sometimes personified as a
    woman ("Lady Wisdom"). What attitude does Wisdom
    have toward fools, in 1:20-33? In 8:1-21 and 9:1-6?
    How would you explain the apparent inconsistency?

8. Sometimes Wisdom is also personified as God's
    helper in the creation of the world (3:19-20; 8:22-
    31). Do you think that this idea violates the
    concept of monotheism? Compare the role of Wisdom
    in 8:22-31 with the role of the Word (Logos) in
    John 1:1-18. In what ways are they similar? In
    what ways are they different?

9. The wise person is instructed to avoid certain
    roadblocks along the path of right living. What
    are these, according to 1:8-19; 2:16-19; 14:5;
    20:23; 23:19-21; 24:23-25? Are these problems that
    can affect any society?

10. Why do you think God disciplines his children,
    according to 3:11-12? For a "commentary" on these
    verses, cf. Hebrews 12:5-11.

11. How is the "fear" of the Lord explained or associ-
    ated with similar concepts in 2:5; 8:13; 9:10;
    15:33?

12. Why does the writer of 6:6-11 point to the ant as a
    model for human life? Do you think this idea ia
    applicable today?

13. The sayings in Proverbs reflect various attitudes

toward material wealth. What are some of these, according to 3:9-10, 13-16; 10:2, 4; 11:24-25, 28; 15:16-17; 16:8; 21:6, 20; 22:1-2, 16; 23:4-5; 28:11; 30:7-9?

14. How is the good wife described in 12:4; 18:22; 19: 14; 31:9-31? This last passage is an acrostic, the first letters of each line forming the alphabet in Hebrew.

15. How should parents bring up children, according to 22:6, 15; 23:13-14? Would you agree with these ideas, or not? Explain.

16. How should one treat the poor and the orphaned, according to 14:31; 22:22-23; 23:10-11? What reasons are given? What reason is given in Deut. 24:17-22? Can you think of an explanation for the difference?

17. How should one treat enemies, according to 24:17-18; 25:21-22? Why?

18. The sayings in Proverbs emphasize the principle of exact retribution - i.e., the good are rewarded, the wicked are punished. Do rewards and punishments come within the present life or in a future life, according to 11:17-21? What do you think is meant by the idea of avoiding death or Sheol, in 15:24; 23:13-14?

19. Hebrew thought often finds a close relationship among inward attitude, spoken word, and outward action. Explain how this is the case in 4:20-27; 6:16-19; 8:13.

20. To what extent do the sayings in Proverbs speak of God's readiness to forgive and restore the wicked? Cf. 3:33-35; 10:29; 14:9, 11; 15:29; 28:13.

32. Ecclesiastes

The word Ecclesiastes represents the Hebrew qoheleth, apparently a "preacher" or "speaker." The author was presumably a wisdom teacher who presents a series of reflections on the meaning of life. The author's critical attitude toward the theory of rewards found in Proverbs, his spirit of individualism, and his familiarity with popular Greek thought all suggest a date in the post-exilic period, perhaps the third century B.C. (Reading: Ecclesiastes.)

1. The opening section, 1:2-11, develops the theme of "vanity." Note that "vanity of vanities" is the Hebrew way of expressing the superlative: "most vain." Do you think that vanity here means "pride" or "futility"? Explain.

2. Does wisdom have any value, according to 1:12-18; 2:12-17; 6:8; 8:16-17; 10:1? Does it have any value, according to 2:13; 7:11-12, 19; 8:1; 9:13-16; 10:12-15? How would you explain these different attitudes toward wisdom? How would you compare them with the view of Proverbs?

3. Does the author find any lasting satisfaction in working to achieve goals and acquire possessions? Cf. 2:1-11, 18-23; 5:10, 13-17.

4. Does the author believe that God exists? Does he think that man can learn about God's actions and purposes? Cf. 3:11; 6:12; 7:14.

5. Does the writer present a cyclical or linear view of history in 1:9-10? How would you compare his outlook with the view of the prophets? With the view of the J and P documents?

6. In 3:2-9, the author defines time by its content – a time for this, a time for that. How would you describe his mood as he reflects on this view of time?

7. Does the author believe that there is justice in human affairs, so that the righteous are rewarded and the wicked are punished? Cf. 3:16; 4:1-3; 5:8-9; 7:15; 8:10, 14; 9:11. How would you compare this with the view of Proverbs (e.g., Prov. 13:21)? Why do you think the author expresses this view?

8. When the author reflects on the fact of human mortality, what does it mean to him? Cf. 2:15-16; 3:19-21; 6:12; 9:1-6.

9. What does the writer think of the underworld

(Sheol), according to 9:10? Does he find any meaning in the idea of continuing existence in Sheol?

10. In Greek thought, the philosophy of Epicureanism advocated the moderate pursuit of pleasure, resulting in a state of well-being for mind and body. The philosophy of Stoicism taught that man should cultivate an attitude of inner serenity amid the changing fortunes of life. Do you find any parallels to these views in 2:24; 3:12-13, 22; 5:18; 6:10-11; 8:15; 9:1, 7; 11:10?

11. Which of the following traditions of Israel's faith does the author refer to: the creation of the world, the covenant with Abraham, the exodus from Egypt, the wandering in the wilderness, the covenant at Sinai, the conquest of Canaan, the covenant with David? Do you think these traditions had any meaning for him? Explain.

12. Some commentators believe that later editors added certain verses to Ecclesiastes to bring the outlook of the book more into line with conventional views of wisdom, rewards, and punishment. Examples are 2:26; 3:17; 7:18b, 26b; 8:11-13; 11:9b; 12:1, 9-11, 12-14. Other interpreters believe that most (at least) of these verses were an original part of the book. How would you assess them?

13. In view of the heading of the book (1:1), Ecclesiastes has often been attributed to king Solomon. How many kings preceded Solomon on the throne in Jerusalem? Do you think Solomon would have written 1:16; 2:7, 9? Why?

14. Which of the following terms do you think are applicable to the author: atheistic, agnostic, sceptical, pious, pensive, cynical, resigned, bitter, pessimistic, melancholy, weary?

15. How would you state the main theme of Ecclesiastes? Can you think of parallels in modern literature? What can we learn from the book today?

33. Job

The main purpose of the book of Job is uncertain:
to answer the question why innocent persons suffer, or
(more probably) to analyze the underlying issue of a
person's relationship to God. The prose beginning
(1:1–2:13) and ending (42:7–17) may represent a traditional story, into which the author has inserted
poetic cycles of dialogue between Job and his visitors.
(Reading: Job 1–14, 38–42).

1. The prologue (1:1–2:13) sets the stage for the
    drama. Note that Satan appears as a member of
    Yahweh's heavenly council or court. What role does
    Satan have? Is he subject to God's control?
    Explain in your own words the question that Satan
    raises about Job (1:9–10). How does Job react
    when he suffers affliction?

2. The poetic sections begin with Job's lament in 3:1–
    26. Does Job react differently here than in the
    prologue? What is the main theme of his lament?
    Compare the thought with Eccles. 4:1–3. How does
    Job think of existence in the underworld, in 3:13–
    15, 17–19?

3. The first visitor, Eliphaz, speaks to Job in 4:1–
    5:27. How does he explain the reason for Job's
    suffering? What verses in particular express his
    view? How would you compare his outlook with that
    of the book of Proverbs (e.g., Prov. 13:21; 14:11)?

4. Job replies in 6:1–7:21. Does he accept Eliphaz'
    explanation for his suffering? Does he regard
    Eliphaz as a comforter or an accuser?

5. The second visitor, Bildad, addresses Job in 8:1–22.
    Does he offer the same explanation as Eliphaz?

6. Job replies in 9:1–10:22. Does he still maintain
    that he is innocent? Whom does he blame for his
    suffering?

7. The third visitor, Zophar, speaks in 11:1–20. Does
    he present the same argument as the others? What
    additional thought does he express in 11:6?

8. Job replies in 12:1–14:22. Does he still maintain his innocence? Does he want to present his case before God? Why can he not do so? Why does he speak of his visitors as "worthless physicians" (13:4)?

9. God speaks to Job out of the whirlwind in 38:1–41:34. Does he try to give a reason for Job's suffering? Why do you think God recounts his works of creation?

10. Job replies to God in 42:1–6. Does he feel reconciled to God at this point? Of what does he repent (42:6)?

11. The prose epilogue (42:7–17) tells of the restoration of Job. Do you think the book would be complete without this ending? Explain.

PART TWO: THE NEW TESTAMENT

1. Aspects of Old Testament Faith

Reading: Exodus 3:1-22; 20:1-17. Amos. Hosea.

1. Exodus 3 describes Moses' encounter with God in the
    burning bush. What does vs. 5 suggest about the
    nature of God? What do vss. 7-9 suggest about God?
    What task does Moses receive? How would you
    explain the meaning of the name Yahweh, according
    to vss. 13-15? (Yahweh, or "Lord," is the special
    Old Testament name for God.)

2. According to Adolf Deissmann, religious experience
    may be "ascending" (in which man finds the way to
    God) or "descending" (in which God comes to man).
    It may result in "union" (in which man merges with
    God) or "communion" (in which man has fellowship
    with God). Which of these terms do you think apply
    to Moses' experience in Exodus 3?

3. In Exodus 20, what is the relation between vs. 2
    and vss. 3-17? Which represents the idea of grace?
    Which represents the idea of law? What does this
    relation indicate about the Old Testament under-
    standing of God?

4. Why do you think the first commandment (vs. 3) is
    given first?

5. The Ten Commandments are part of the Sinai covenant,
    made with the whole people of Israel. Yet the
    commandments themselves are in the singular ("thou
    shalt..."). Why is it significant that they are
    addressed to individual persons?

6. The prophet Amos was active about 750 B.C. Analyze
    his sermonette in 1:3-2:16. Under what conditions
    had the surrounding nations done wrong? Does Amos
    believe that Yahweh's power extends over these other
    nations? Under what conditions had Judah and Israel
    done wrong? How do you think the audience reacted
    up to 2:4? After 2:4? How would you state the
    main idea of this passage?

7. Amos was especially concerned to apply the tradition of the exodus from Egypt to his own day. What meanings does he find in this tradition in 2:10; 3:1-2; 9:7? Do you think these meanings are still applicable today?

8. Summarize the criticisms that Amos makes of his society in 3:15; 5:10-12; 6:4-7; 8:4-6. What areas of life do these represent? Is "religion" for Amos a separate category of life or a way of living in all areas of life?

9. What is Amos' attitude toward religious ceremony and ritual in 4:4-5; 5:21-24? Does he want to abolish ritual or reform it? Explain.

10. The prophet Hosea was active about 745 B.C. What meaning does he find in the tradition of the exodus from Egypt, according to 9:10; 11:1, 3-4; 13:4? How does he depict God in 11:1? How does he describe God in 13:4?

11. The word "controversy" in Hosea 4:1 could also be translated "lawsuit." In what ways does Hosea 4:1-3 resemble a lawsuit? Who are the plaintiff and the defendants? What are the charges? What set of laws does 4:2 remind you of? How would you relate 4:1b to 4:2?

12. How would you summarize the underlying cause of the people's wrongdoing, according to Hosea 6:4, 6; 10:12; 13:4-6?

13. In 2:14-15, Hosea speaks of the valley of Achor, near the northwestern part of the Dead Sea, close to the route by which the Israelites first entered Canaan about 500 years earlier. What do you think he is saying in this passage?

14. Sometimes it is said that in the Old Testament, God is a God of law, but in the New Testament a God of love. How correct do you think this is?

15. How would you compare the Old Testament view of history with the modern idea of progress and the Marxist view of history?

2. The Genealogies and Birth Narratives

Reading: Matt. 1:1–2:23. Lk. 1:1–2:52; 3:23–38.

1. Matthew's genealogy of Jesus begins with Abraham (Matt. 1:2). Why do you think this was important for Matthew? The genealogy also includes king David (Matt. 1:6). Why was this significant?

2. Notice that Luke's genealogy is in the reverse order (Lk. 3:23–28). It also includes David and Abraham, but then goes back to Adam. Whom does Adam represent? Why do you think it was important for Luke to trace the genealogy to Adam?

3. Which genealogy occasionally mentions women? Do you know who Ruth was?

4. Many Jews believed that the Messiah would be a descendant of David. What did Jesus say about this belief, according to Matt. 22:41–46?

5. Do the genealogies actually say that Joseph was the father of Jesus? Cf. Matt. 1:16; Lk. 3:23. What would be the purpose of including genealogies?

6. According to Matt. 1:18–25, to whom does an angel appear to announce the birth of Jesus? According to Lk. 1:26–38, to whom does the angel appear? Can you think of an explanation for this difference? The name Jesus comes from the Hebrew word yasha, "save." Which writer is aware of this derivation?

7. Compare Matt. 2:1–2 with Lk. 2:1–20. Which writer mentions the shepherds? Which one mentions the wise men? Which says that Jesus was born in a house? Which says he was born in a manger?

8. Which writer is especially concerned to interpret events connected with the birth of Jesus as the fulfillment of Old Testament sayings? Which is concerned to show that Jesus and John the Baptist were related?

9. What kinds of things does God do, according to the Magnificat (Lk. 1:46–55)? What will John the Baptist do, according to the Benedictus (Lk. 1:68–

79)? What is the scope of the salvation that Jesus will bring, according to the <u>Nunc</u> <u>Dimittis</u> (Lk. 2:29-32)?

10. What beliefs about Jesus are reflected in Lk. 2:41-52? Apart from this passage, does the New Testament give any other information about the boyhood of Jesus? Why?

11. Why do you think Mark has no genealogy or nativity narrative?

3. The Baptism and Temptation Narratives

Reading: Matt. 3:1-4:11. Mk. 1:1-13. Lk. 3:1-22; 4:1-13.

1. What were the main themes of John the Baptist's preaching? Was he influenced by eschatological thought? Why did he tell Jewish listeners that it was useless to claim descent from Abraham (cf. Matt. 3:7-10; Lk. 3:7-9)?

2. Compare Matt. 3:3; Mk. 1:3; and Lk. 3:4-6. What does the Old Testament quotation suggest about the role of John the Baptist? Why do you think Luke extends the quotation? Note that Lk. 3:6 is not in the Hebrew Bible but is in the Septuagint. What does this suggest about Luke?

3. Compare the description of John in Matt. 3:4 and Mk. 1:6 with the description of Elijah in II Kings 1:8. Why do you think the early Christians would make this comparison? See Malachi 4:5-6 and Matt. 17:9-13.

4. Did John regard himself as the Messiah?

5. What form of baptism did John use? Why do you think the church later used other forms as well?

6. What do you think it meant to Jesus to be baptized? Since Jesus was sinless, how could he receive a baptism for the forgiveness of sins? How does Matthew deal with this problem, in 3:13-15?

7. Compare Mk. 1:11 ("Thou art my beloved Son") with Ps. 2:7. Ps. 2 was an ancient hymn for the coronation of the Davidic king, later apparently applied to the messianic king to come in the future. What do these words suggest as they are applied to Jesus?

8. Compare Mk. 1:11 ("with thee I am well pleased") with Is. 42:1. This section of the book of Isaiah speaks of the "servant" of the Lord who suffers on behalf of others. What do the words suggest with reference to Jesus?

9. Compare Mk. 1:11 and Matt. 3:17. Do you think Matthew might have changed Mark's wording? Why?

10. Why do you think the temptation accounts, in all three synoptics, immediately follow the baptism accounts? Why do you think Mark has a very brief account, while Matthew and Luke have longer accounts? Can you think of any reason why the order differs in Matthew and Luke?

11. Following Matthew's account (4:1-11), explain in your own words the meaning of the temptation that Jesus faced. Was it irreverent for the early Christians to think of Jesus as being tempted? Cf. Hebrews 2:17-18; 4:15; 5:8.

4. The Ministry in Galilee (1)

Reading: Matt. 4:12-7:29. Mk. 1:14-39. Lk. 4:14-5:11; 6:20-49.

1. How old was Jesus when he began his ministry, according to Luke (3:23)?

2. What were the main themes of Jesus' preaching, according to the summary in Mk. 1:15? Is the "kingdom of God" here viewed as imminent or already present?

3. Who were the first four disciples that Jesus called to follow him? What part of the country were they from? What was their occupation?

70

4. Mk. 1:21-39 describes Jesus' visit to Capernaum.
   What kinds of activities did he engage in on this
   day? What is meant by his "authority" in 1:22?
   What is the significance of "that evening, at sun-
   down," in 1:32? What do you think he prayed about,
   according to 1:35? How does Mark summarize this
   part of his ministry, in 1:39? How does Matthew
   expand and generalize this summary (Matt. 4:23)?

5. What do you think the miraculous catch of fish
   symbolizes, in Lk. 5:1-11?

6. Matthew's Sermon on the Mount (Matt. 5-7) has a
   parallel in Luke's Sermon on the Plain (Lk. 6:20-
   49). Which is longer? Do they begin and end in
   the same way? Why do you think the mountain was
   significant for Matthew? Who in the Old Testament
   had brought down a law from a mountain?

7. Note the Beatitudes in Matt. 5:3-12. Why are they
   called Beatitudes? What does the first clause in
   each Beatitude describe? What does the second
   clause indicate? Do you think the Beatitudes
   describe eight kinds of disciples or eight aspects
   of discipleship? Are the rewards of discipleship
   present or future, or both?

8. Would you characterize the Beatitudes as promises
   to the disciples, descriptions of the disciples, or
   both? Of what person do the Beatitudes remind you?

9. Jesus presumably addressed the Beatitudes to Jewish
   people, since he had few contacts with other people
   in Palestine. Do the Beatitudes themselves indicate
   that discipleship is limited to any particular
   group?

10. What do you think it means to be "poor in spirit"?
    Note that Luke (6:20) has simply "poor." Which do
    you think is original? In Matthew's fourth
    Beatitude, do you think that "righteousness" refers
    to human standards of action or to the deliverance
    that God brings, or both?

11. Why did Jesus compare his disciples to salt (Matt.
    5:13)? How can they be the light of the world
    (Matt. 5:14)? Compare Matt. 5:15 with Lk. 11:33.
    Who benefits from the light, in each case?

12. Note the six contrasts or antitheses in Matt. 5:21-

46, and compare them with the Ten Commandments in Exodus 20:3-17. Do you think Jesus wanted his followers to observe the Ten Commandments? Which antitheses refer to them? Did Jesus make the Old Testament law more rigorous or less? What do you think he implied with the words "but I say to you"?

13. The principle of "an eye for an eye" (Matt. 5:38; cf. Exodus 21:24) was originally intended to place a limit on retaliation; in Jesus' time it had been generally replaced by a system of fines. How did Jesus treat this topic? Is his teaching easy or difficult to follow?

14. With Matt. 5:43 compare Leviticus 19:17-18. Did the Old Testament command hatred of enemies? (Note, however, that this injunction appears in the writings of the Dead Sea community.) How did Jesus treat this topic? Do you think that it is possible to follow his teaching?

15. In Matt. 6:1-18, Jesus comments on the religious practices of almsgiving, prayer, and fasting. What does he want his followers to avoid, when they engage in these practices? Note that in each case he says, "and your Father who sees in secret will reward you." Are these activities worthwhile for their own sake? How should the disciples of Jesus think of rewards in this connection?

16. Why are people anxious, according to Matt. 6:25-34? What advice did Jesus give? Did he mean that people should not plan for the future?

17. What kind of judgments do you think Jesus prohibited in Matt. 7:1-5?

18. What is an a fortiori argument? How did Jesus use this argument in his teaching on prayer, in Matt. 7:7-11? (Jewish rabbis spoke of this type of reasoning as "from light to heavy.")

19. What is the test of a good person, according to Matt. 7:15-20?

20. How would you explain the meaning of the concluding parable, in Matt. 7:24-27? If the Beatitudes suggest that the kingdom of God is a gift, does this parable contradict that idea?

5. The Ministry in Galilee (2)

Reading: Matt. 8:1-10:42. Mk. 1:40-2:22. Lk. 5:12-39.

1. Note that in chs. 5-7, Matthew gives a collection
    of Jesus' teachings; in chs. 8-9, he gives a series
    of ten "mighty works" or miracles of Jesus. What
    do these chapters all together indicate about
    Matthew's understanding of Jesus?

2. What was a centurion (Matt. 8:5-13)? Was he a Jew
    or a Gentile? Note that most Jews considered it a
    religious offense to enter the house of a Gentile.
    Did Jesus share this view? What do you think Jesus
    meant by "faith" in vs. 10? What do you think is
    the main point of this passage?

3. As part of the account of the centurion's servant,
    Matthew includes two verses comparing the kingdom
    of God to a banquet (Matt. 8:11-12; Luke has a
    similar passage, but in a different context). Do
    these verses refer to the present or the future
    aspect of the kingdom? Who are the "many" who will
    come "from east and west"? Who are the "sons of
    the kingdom" who will be excluded?

4. Compare Matt. 8:16-17 with Mk. 1:32-34. How does
    each writer conclude the passage? Can you explain
    how these endings reflect characteristic interests
    of Matthew and Mark?

5. In the account of the healing of the paralytic
    (Mk. 2:1-12), what criticism is made of Jesus? How
    does he deal with it? In popular Jewish thought,
    illness was regarded as punishment for sin. How
    does the account reflect this belief? There is
    apparently no evidence in Judaism for the idea that
    the Messiah would be endowed with the power to
    forgive sins; only God could do so. In light of
    this, what does the incident imply about the nature
    of Jesus?

6. According to Mk. 2:13-17, Jesus ate with tax collec-
    tors and sinners. Would pious Jews do this? How
    did he explain his action? This incident may
    utilize the imagery of the banquet as a symbol for
    the kingdom of God. Does it refer to the present or

the future aspect of the kingdom? What does the symbolism mean here?

7. Compare Matt. 6:16-18 with Matt. 9:14-17. What does each passage say about the practice of fasting? Note that the second passage reflects the Jewish custom of suspending fasting regulations during the time of a wedding celebration. What does Jesus mean in referring to this custom?

8. Matthew gives a list of Jesus' twelve disciples in 10:1-4. What do you think the number twelve may symbolize?

9. Why did Jesus send out the disciples on a mission of their own, according to Matt. 10:5-16? Where were they to go? What were they to take? Compare Matt. 10:9-10 with Mk. 6:8-9.

10. What view of history is reflected in Matt. 10:23? Is the term Son of Man used here with regard to the present or the future? How is it used in Matt. 8:20? (Although Matt. 10:23 has no parallel in the other synoptics, Albert Schweitzer emphasized this verse in his analysis of Jesus' outlook.)

11. Compare Matt. 10:34-36 with Lk. 12:51-53. Do you think that these verses indicate the purpose or the result of Jesus' mission? What is the meaning of "sword" in Matthew's form of this passage (cf. the reading in Luke)? Does Christian faith necessarily lead to divisions in families? Does this sometimes happen?

12. How would you explain the meaning of Matt. 10:39?

6. The Ministry in Galilee (3)

Reading: Matt. 11:1-12:50. Mk. 2:23-3:35. Lk. 6:1-8:3.

1. According to Matt. 11:2-6, John the Baptist wanted to know who Jesus was. Why do you think Jesus did not give a direct answer to the question? How would you explain the meaning of his reply? Why might some people "take offense" at Jesus?

2. What did Jesus think of John the Baptist, according to Matt. 11:7-19? Why would he compare him to Elijah (cf. Malachi 4:5-6)?

3. What do you think Jesus meant when he said that the kingdom of heaven "has suffered violence" or "has been coming violently" (Matt. 11:12)?

4. Which of the cities mentioned in Lk. 10:13-15 were Jewish? Which were Gentile? What does the passage suggest about Jesus' expectations concerning the Jewish people of his time?

5. What does Matt. 11:25-30 indicate about Jesus' relation to God, Jesus' function in revealing God, and Jesus' relation to his disciples?

6. According to Deuteronomy 23:25, was a person allowed to gather grain from a field? How then did Jesus' disciples offend the Pharisees, in Mk. 2:23-28? How did Jesus justify their actions?

7. Why do you think Jesus offended the Pharisees when he healed the man with a withered hand, in Mk. 3:1-6?

8. Review the five "controversy stories" that Mark presents in 2:1-3:6. What aspects and activities of Jesus' ministry do these incidents depict? From what group did the main opposition to Jesus come?

9. According to Mk. 3:14-15, Jesus appointed the twelve disciples for three reasons. On the basis of these, how would you describe the purpose of the church today?

10. The account of the widow's son at Nain (Lk. 7:11-17) is one of two synoptic accounts in which Jesus restores a person to life. The other is the incident concerning Jairus' daughter, Matt. 9:18-26. What do these accounts reveal about God's will for human life? How would you relate them to the incidents in which Jesus heals illnesses?

11. The account of the woman with the ointment (Lk. 7:36-50) incorporates the parable of the two debtors. The account and the parable both deal with the relationship between love and forgiveness. How

does each present this relationship? Is there any
inconsistency? What do you think Jesus was trying
to illustrate to his host, Simon the Pharisee?

12. The accusation against Jesus in Mk. 3:19-27 reflects
the first-century belief in evil spirits, led by
Satan (or Beelzebub, "lord of the dwelling"). How
does Jesus refute the charge that he is acting in
collusion with evil spirits?

13. Compare Matt. 12:38-42 with Lk. 11:29-32. In these
passages Jesus refuses to give any sign to authen-
ticate his mission except "the sign of Jonah."
What two meanings are given to this sign in
Matthew's account? What meaning does it have in
Luke's account? On the basis of these passages,
what answer would you give to people today when they
ask for a "sign" or "proof" that Jesus was the
Messiah?

14. Who belongs to the "family" of Jesus, according to
Mk. 3:31-35? Is Jesus' definition applicable to
all persons or restricted to a particular group?

7. The Ministry in Galilee (4)

Reading: Matt. 13:1-15:39. Mk. 4:1-8:10. Lk. 8:4-9:17.

1. Why did Jesus use parables, according to Mk. 4:10-
12? Do you think this passage gives the purpose or
the result of the use of parables? How would you
compare this passage with Mk. 4:21-25?

2. The parable of the sower, Mk. 4:1-9, may reflect
Jesus' own experience in preaching the kingdom of
God, as well as the advice that he gave to his
disciples. Do you think the parable indicates that
Jesus was pessimistic or optimistic about the
results of preaching?

3. What do you think it is that the disciples of Jesus
can see and hear, according to Matt. 13:16-17? Do
followers of Jesus in later centuries have the same
opportunity?

4. What aspect of the kingdom of God is depicted by

the parable of the seed growing secretly, Mk. 4:26-29? In what sense is this a parable of hope and encouragement?

5. Several interpretations of the parable of the mustard seed, Mk. 4:30-32, are possible - the gradual growth of God's rule in the life of the individual person, the gradual spread of God's kingdom throughout society, the contrast between the apparently insignificant beginnings of the kingdom in Jesus' ministry and the unexpected results of his ministry. Which interpretation do you think is correct? Why?

6. The "birds of the air" may be an allegorical touch in the parable of the mustard seed. On the basis of the imagery in Daniel 4:19-22, what do you think the birds may symbolize?

7. Compare the three accounts of the stilling of the storm in Matt. 8:23-27; Mk. 4:35-41; Lk. 8:22-25. What title do the disciples use to address Jesus in each of the three accounts? Which title is most meaningful as an expression of Christian faith? Which account emphasizes the importance of discipleship by saying that the disciples "followed" Jesus? Which account emphasizes the importance of faith by introducing the discussion of faith before the stilling of the storm? Which account presents the story not simply as an incident in the life of Jesus but also as a vignette of life in the early church?

8. According to Psalms 89:9 and 107:23-32, who stills the raging of the sea? In light of this, what does the account of the stilling of the storm indicate about Jesus?

9. The parables of the weeds and the net occur only in the gospel of Matthew (13:24-30, 47-50). Some interpreters believe that Matthew understands them in relation to problems in the church of his day. What do you think this would indicate about Matthew's understanding of the church?

10. The twin parables of the hidden treasure and the pearl, Matt. 13:44-46, probably have the same main point. What do you think they are saying about the kingdom of God? How would you state this idea in

relation to life today?

11. Mark's account of the rejection at Nazareth (6:1-6) gives some information about Jesus and his family. What was his occupation? Did he have brothers and sisters? Why do you think the people of Nazareth took offense at Jesus? Why do you think "he could do no mighty work there"?

12. Luke's account of the rejection at Nazareth (4:16-30) has a slightly different emphasis. What scriptural passage did Jesus apply to himself, according to Lk. 4:16-21? Why do you think Jesus referred to Elijah and Elisha, according to Lk. 4:25-30?

13. The feeding of the 5,000 is the only miracle related in all four gospels; read Mark's account in 6:30-44. Explain which of the following interpretations you think are appropriate: a) Jesus performed a nature miracle by multiplying the loaves and fish; b) by giving an example of sharing, Jesus inspired others in the crowd to share food which they had brought with them; c) the story illustrates Jesus' concern (and the church's concern) for the material well-being of persons; d) because some words are reminiscent of the Last Supper ("taking... looked... blessed... broke... gave"), the account indicates that the celebration of the Lord's Supper was intended for all the followers of Jesus, not just the twelve; e) the account utilizes the imagery of the meal as a symbol for the kingdom of God; f) the incident shows that Jesus had similar, but greater, powers than the Old Testament prophet Elisha (cf. II Kings 4:42-44).

14. Compare the two accounts of Jesus' walking on the water in Matt. 14:22-33 and Mk. 6:45-52. Who walked "through the sea," according to Psalm 77:19-20? When? In light of this, what do you think the gospel accounts are saying about Jesus? What do you think is the point of the incident concerning Peter in Matthew's account? How would you compare the endings of the two accounts?

15. Compare the account of the centurion's servant (Matt. 8:5-13) with the story of the Syrophoenician woman (Mk. 7:24-30). In what ways are they similar? How are they different?

8. The Ministry in Galilee (5)

Reading: Matt. 16:1-18:35. Mk. 8:11-9:50. Lk. 9:18-50.

1. Read Mark's account of Peter's confession at
    Caesarea Philippi (Mk. 8:27-33). Who did Peter
    believe that Jesus was? What events did Jesus
    expect to happen? What Jewish groups would be
    opposed to him? Did Peter understand what Jesus
    was saying?

2. Read Matthew's account of Peter's confession (Matt.
    16:13-23). Note that the special charge to Peter
    (Matt. 16:17-19) has no parallel in the other
    gospels. What do you think is meant by "on this
    rock" in vs. 18? What authority will Peter have,
    according to vs. 19?

3. What are the conditions of discipleship, according
    to Mk. 8:34-38? How would you state these in terms
    of life today?

4. The account of the transfiguration of Jesus (Mk. 9:
    2-8) mentions a mountain at which God is present.
    Does this remind you of an event in the Old Testa-
    ment? Can you guess what Moses and Elijah may
    represent? The cloud (vs. 7) symbolizes God's
    glory and presence; according to Jewish thought,
    the cloud would reappear in the messianic age.
    What do you think it signifies here?

5. What do you think Jesus meant when he told his
    disciples that they must become like children in
    order to enter the kingdom of God (Matt. 18:1-5)?

6. The expression "little ones" in Matt. 18:6 may refer
    to members of the church, little children, or the
    ordinary people of the time. In each case, how
    would Jesus want his disciples to treat such
    persons?

7. Why did Jesus accept the work of the strange ex-
    orcist, according to Lk. 9:49-50? Can you think
    of examples today of persons or institutions that
    do God's work even though they are not specifically
    Christian? Do you think there is any inconsistency
    between Lk. 9:50 and Lk. 11:23?

8. Compare Matt. 16:18-19 (in which "you" is singular) with Matt. 18:18 (in which "you" is plural). Whom is Jesus addressing in each case? Note that in the four gospels, the word "church" (ekklesia) appears only in Matt. 16:18 and 18:17.

9. Some Jewish rabbis said that a person should be willing to forgive three times; others said seven times. What was Jesus' teaching on forgiveness, according to Matt. 18:21-22?

10. The parable of the unmerciful servant (Matt. 18:23-25) tells of two men who had debts of ten thousand talents (about ten million dollars) and a hundred denarii (about twenty dollars). Does the parable indicate that we forgive others so that God will forgive us, or that God forgives us so that we can forgive others? How would you relate this parable to the petition for forgiveness in the Lord's Prayer?

9. Luke's Special Section (1)

Reading: Lk. 9:51-13:35.

1. When Jewish people traveled from Galilee to Jerusalem, they usually crossed to the eastern side of the Jordan river to avoid going through Samaria. Luke and John, however, indicate that Jesus went through Samaria. According to Lk. 9:51-56, how did the Samaritan people react to Jesus? What attitude did he have toward them?

2. The sending out of the seventy disciples appears only in Luke (10:1-20). Why do you think Luke has this, in addition to the mission of the twelve disciples? Note that in ancient Jewish thought, seventy was the traditional number of the Gentile nations in the world. What does Lk. 10:18 suggest about Jesus' view of history? How would you correlate this with Lk. 10:9?

3. The parable of the good Samaritan occurs only in Luke (10:29-37). How do you think a Jewish audience would react when Jesus made a Samaritan the hero of

the parable? Did the parable answer the question? Explain. How would you tell a present-day version of this parable?

4. If the parable of the good Samaritan is treated strictly as a parable, it has one main point. How would you state this? If it is interpreted as an allegory, then each detail can symbolize something else. Note the following points in the interpretation by Augustine (ca. A.D. 400): the man who went down from Jerusalem to Jericho is Adam; Jerusalem is the heavenly city of peace, from whose blessedness Adam fell; the thieves are the devil and his angels; "stripped him" means that they took away Adam's immortality; the Samaritan is Christ himself; the inn is the church; the innkeeper is the apostle Paul. This kind of interpretation prevailed for many centuries. Do you think the story of the good Samaritan should be treated as a parable or an allegory? Why?

5. What do you think is the main point of the parable of the friend at midnight, Lk. 11:5-8? How can this parable be misunderstood?

6. Does Jesus speak of the kingdom of God as present or future in Lk. 11:20 (cf. Matt. 12:28)? Compare this viewpoint with Luke 10:9 and 10:18.

7. Is it possible today to think of the kingdom of God as present and as still to come? Explain.

8. What criticisms did Jesus make of the Pharisees and the lawyers (scribes), according to Lk. 11:37-12:1? Can you think of modern parallels to these criticisms?

9. Jewish rabbis often served as arbitrators in legal disputes. In the parable of the rich fool (Lk. 12:13-21), Jesus refuses this role. Why do you think he refused? Why is the rich man in the parable described as a fool? In what way was he rich? In what way should he be rich?

10. The saying in Lk. 12:32 occurs only in Luke. Who are the "little flock"? Is the kingdom a gift from God or a reward for human achievement?

11. The parable of the fig tree (Lk. 13:6-9) occurs only

in Luke. What does the fig tree represent (cf. Hosea 9:10)? What do you think is the point of the parable? Is the parable one of warning, or hope, or both?

12. According to Lk. 13:22-30, did Jesus think that everyone would enter the kingdom of God? Who would be excluded? Who (implicitly) would be able to enter?

13. Compare questions 10 and 12 above. If the kingdom is a gift, why are human actions important?

10. Luke's Special Section (2)

Reading: Lk. 14:1-18:14.

1. Jewish tradition prohibited healing on the sabbath except in cases of extreme emergency. Why did the Pharisees object to Jesus' action, in Lk. 14:1-6? What kind of reasoning did Jesus use to explain his action (cf. Topic 4, question 18)?

2. Why did Jesus tell the Pharisee to invite "the poor, the maimed, the lame, the blind" when he gave a feast (Lk. 14:12-14)? Note that in one of the Dead Sea Scrolls these people are mentioned, in almost identical words, as persons who will be excluded from the messianic banquet in the future.

3. Note that in Lk. 14:14, Jesus refers to rewards as a motive for conduct. Compare Topic 4, question 15. Do you think Jesus regarded the expectation of reward as the only motive that his followers should have for their actions? Explain.

4. The parable of the great supper in Lk. 14:15-24 utilizes the imagery of the banquet as a symbol for the kingdom of God (cf. Topic 5, questions 3 and 6). How many groups of people are invited to the banquet? Whom do you think each group represents? Which groups are admitted to the banquet? How do you think Luke understood this parable as a paradigm for the mission of the early church?

5. Compare the parable of the great supper (Lk. 14:15-

24) with Matthew's parable of the marriage feast (Matt. 22:1-10). How many groups of people are mentioned in Matthew's parable? Whom do they represent? How do you think Matthew understood this parable as an interpretation of the destruction of Jerusalem by the Romans in A.D. 70?

6. Compare the parables of the lost sheep and the lost coin (Lk. 15:1-10). Note the similarities: each stresses the ideas of searching for something lost, the value of what was lost, and the joy of recovering it. Note also the differences: the sheep was lost outside the fold, and the coin was lost within the house; the sheep was lost because of its own ignorance, and the coin was lost because of the owner's carelessness. In interpreting these parables, would you stress the similarities or the differences? Why?

7. The parable of the prodigal son (Lk. 15:11-32) may perhaps be called the parable of the two lost sons. In what sense was each son "lost"? In what sense would the elder son resemble the Pharisees of Jesus' day? In what sense could he resemble Christians today?

8. The parable of the rich man and Lazarus (Lk. 16:19-31) reflects a current Jewish view of the underworld as a place where the spirits of the dead received rewards or punishments. How would you explain the parable as a) a criticism of materialistic Jews such as the Sadducees; b) a criticism of Jews who did not believe in Jesus?

9. The parable of the farmer and the servant (Lk. 17:7-10) reflects everyday conditions of life in Palestine in Jesus' day. Do you think the meaning is a) the kingdom of God is a reward for faithful performance of duty; or b) the kingdom is a gift which cannot be earned by human achievement?

10. Jesus' saying about the kingdom of God in Lk. 17:20-21 may be interpreted in several ways: a) the kingdom of God is "within you," i.e., God's rule is a new spiritual principle already operative in the hearts and lives of people; b) the kingdom of God is "in the midst of you," i.e., when the kingdom comes, it will come with dramatic suddenness as a new world order or world age; c) the kingdom of God

is "in the midst of you," i.e., the kingdom is already at least partially present through the person and ministry of Jesus himself. How would you understand the saying? Why?

11. The Judean Section (1)

Reading: Matt. 19:1-21:32. Mk. 10:1-11:33. Lk. 18:15-20:8.

1. According to Mk. 10:17-31, what did the rich young man want to receive? What commandments did Jesus remind him of? What did Jesus ask him to do in addition? Do you think that Jesus would have asked all his followers to give away their possessions, or was he giving this advice only to the rich young man? Explain. Why do you think Jesus said it was so difficult for the wealthy to enter the kingdom of God?

2. The parable of the laborers in the vineyard (Matt. 20:1-16) reflects conditions in first-century Palestine, in which workers were hired on a day-to-day basis. The day lasted from about 6 a.m. to 6 p.m.; the eleventh hour (vs. 6) would be about 5 p.m. Do you think the vineyard owner was fair to those who had worked all day? What do you think the parable indicates about the basis on which God admits persons into his kingdom?

3. The parable of the laborers in the vineyard occurs only in Matthew, and the parable of the prodigal son occurs only in Luke (15:11-32). How would you compare these two parables?

4. What question do James and John ask Jesus, according to Mk. 10:35-45? In his reply, how does Jesus describe true greatness? Note that the Greek word translated "ransom" occurs in the Gospels only in Mk. 10:45 and its parallel in Matt. 20:28. The word literally means a price paid for the deliverance of a person or a thing; here it seems to signify the redemptive significance of Jesus' life. The language is reminiscent of Isaiah 52:13-53:12. Do you think that Jesus could have been influenced by

this passage?

5. The incident involving Zacchaeus occurs only in Luke (19:1-10). The meal that Jesus shared in Zacchaeus' house may reflect the imagery of the messianic banquet (cf. Topic 5, questions 3, 6; Topic 10, questions 2, 4). Do you think that Zacchaeus received salvation because he repented and accepted God's grace, or because he performed certain good works? Explain.

6. The "triumphal entry" of Jesus into Jerusalem on Palm Sunday is related in Matt. 21:1-9. In the Roman empire, a triumph was a procession led by a victorious general returning to Rome with spoils of war. How does Matthew depict Jesus on this occasion? Note especially the quotation from Zechariah 9:9 in Matt. 21:5.

7. Mark's account of Jesus' entry into Jerusalem (Mk. 11:1-10) suggests that the people regarded Jesus as a political messiah who would establish a Jewish state (cf. especially vs. 10). Was this Jesus' intention, or did the people misunderstand him?

8. The cursing of the fig tree (Matt. 21:18-19; Mk. 11: 12-14) presents difficulties in interpretation. Whom do you think the fig tree represents (cf. Hosea 9:10)? Some commentators suggest that the incident is a dramatized form of the parable of the fig tree in Lk. 13:6-9 (cf. Topic 9, question 11). What is the main point of this parable? How does the cursing of the fig tree shift the emphasis of Luke's parable?

9. Several interpretations have been proposed to explain the cleansing of the temple (Matt. 21:12-13; Mk. 11:15-19; Lk. 19:45-48): Jesus opposed the practices of changing money and selling animals in the temple precincts; Jesus protested against excessive greed on the part of the money-changers and merchants; Jesus protested against the sacrificial system itself; Jesus protested against the use of the Court of the Gentiles for commercial activities, since this court was to be reserved for non-Jews to worship God. Which interpretation do you think is correct? Which account gives most support to the fourth interpretation?

10. The parable of the two sons appears in Matt. 21:28-

32. How would you compare this parable with those of the laborers in the vineyard and the prodigal son (cf. above, questions 2 and 3)?

12. The Judean Section (2)

Reading: Matt. 21:33-25:46. Mk. 12:1-13:37. Lk. 20:9-21:38.

1. The parable of the wicked tenants appears in Mk. 12:1-12. Review the treatment of "parable" and "allegory" in Topic 9, question 4. Would you regard the story of the wicked tenants as a parable or an allegory? Who is represented by the owner of the vineyard, the tenants, the servants, and the son? What effect did this story have on the Jewish leaders?

2. What did Jesus say about the obligations that people owed the Roman state, according to Mk. 12:13-17? What did he say about their obligations toward God? Which did he regard as more important?

3. The Sadducees did not believe in resurrection because they accepted only the first five books of the Old Testament as authoritative and they could not find the idea of resurrection in these books. Why do you think they asked Jesus about resurrection, according to Mk. 12:18-27? Did Jesus himself believe in resurrection? (For the difference between the Sadducees and the Pharisees on this issue, cf. Acts 23:6-8.)

4. Jewish teachers sometimes formulated short summaries of the essential meaning of the Jewish law. The scribe who asked Jesus about the most important commandment was seeking such a summary (Mk. 12:28-34). From which Old Testament passages did Jesus quote in giving his summary? Whom do you think he meant by "neighbor"?

5. Many Jewish people believed that the Messiah would be a descendant of David who would restore the Jewish state as it had been in David's time. According to Mk. 12:35-37, what was Jesus' attitude

toward the Davidic descent of the Messiah? Do you think that he was trying to deny his own Davidic descent or indicate that his understanding of messiahship was different from the usual Jewish view? Explain.

6. The Jerusalem temple was destroyed by the Romans in A.D. 70, about forty years after Jesus' death. Why do you think he expected that this would happen, according to Mk. 13:1-4? If Jesus was referring to the destruction of Jerusalem in Mk. 13:30, was his estimate of time correct?

7. The "desolating sacrilege" or "abomination of desolation" in Mk. 13:14 reflects a phrase in Daniel 9:27, which referred to the altar of Zeus erected by Antiochus Epiphanes in 168 B.C. on the site of the altar of burnt offering at the Jerusalem temple. In Mark, the phrase may refer to the order of the Roman emperor Caligula about A.D. 41 that his statue be set up in the temple. Mark may also be thinking of the Roman destruction of Jerusalem in A.D. 70. What does Luke think of at this point (Lk. 21:20)?

8. The parable of the ten maidens in Matt. 25:1-13 emphasizes that a person should make preparation in time so that he will not be too late for the kingdom of God. How would you compare this parable with the parable of the laborers in the vineyard (Topic 11, question 2)?

9. The parable of the talents in Matt. 25:14-30 reflects the meaning of "talent" as an amount of silver or gold worth about $1,000. Jesus may originally have directed the parable against Jewish leaders of the time who had not made productive use of the spiritual gifts entrusted to them. How would you explain the meaning of the parable in modern terms?

10. The parable of the last judgment in Matt. 25:31-46 may refer especially to the "nations" or "Gentiles," i.e., non-Jewish peoples who did not know of Jesus or his message. By what criteria will these people be admitted into the kingdom of God in the future? What does the parable suggest about the responsibility of Christians in the world today?

13. The Last Supper and the Trial

Reading: Matt. 26:1–27:26. Mk. 14:1–15:15. Lk. 22:1–
23:25.

1. Mk. 14:3–9 tells of the woman who poured ointment
   on Jesus' head as he sat at table. (This woman
   was Mary, the sister of Martha, if John is relating
   the same incident in John 12:1–8.) Why do you think
   the woman did this? How did Jesus interpret the
   significance of her deed?

2. The decision of Judas to betray Jesus is related in
   Matt. 26:14–16; Mk. 14:10–11; Lk. 22:3–6. With
   whom did Judas negotiate? Do any of these accounts
   indicate why Judas decided to betray Jesus? What
   do you think the reason was?

3. Read the accounts of the Last Supper in Matt. 26:26–
   29 and Mk. 14:22–25. Are they essentially the same?
   Why do you think Jesus wanted to share this meal
   with his disciples? What do you think he meant by
   connecting the bread with his body, and the wine
   with his blood?

4. Notice the imagery of the meal as a symbol for the
   kingdom of God in Matt. 26:29 and Mk. 14:25. Is
   the kingdom of God presented here in its present or
   its future aspect? Can you think of examples in
   which Jesus used this symbolism previously in his
   ministry?

5. Luke's account of the Last Supper includes some of
   the last words that Jesus spoke to his disciples
   (Lk. 22:21–38). What did Jesus say to help them
   carry on after his death? What do you think Jesus
   meant when he advised his disciples to buy swords?

6. What did Jesus pray for in Gethsemane, according to
   Mk. 14:32–42? What do you think he meant when he
   told the disciples to pray that they might not enter
   into temptation?

7. When Jesus was brought before the high priest, he
   was accused of threatening to destroy the temple
   (Mk. 14:57–58). Is this what Jesus had said,
   according to Mk. 13:1–4? Jesus was also accused

88

of uttering blasphemy (Mk. 14:63-64). Had he done
so, according to Leviticus 24:16?

8. What had Jesus predicted about Peter, according to
   Mk. 14:29-31? Did this come true, according to
   Mk. 14:66-72?

9. What did Judas do with the thirty pieces of silver,
   according to Matt. 27:3-10? How did he die? (For
   another account, cf. Acts 1:18-19.)

10. When Jesus was brought before Pilate, what did
    Pilate ask him (Mk. 15:2)? Why would Pilate ask
    this question? Do the accounts of the hearing
    before Pilate indicate that Pilate found Jesus
    guilty of any crime deserving death?

14. Death and Resurrection

Reading: Matt. 27:27-28:20. Mk. 15:16-16:8. Lk. 23:26-
24:53.

1. When Jesus was crucified, what charge was placed on
   the inscription (Mk. 15:26)? Was this a religious
   or a political charge?

2. What special account does Luke give of the two
   criminals who were executed with Jesus (Lk. 23:39-
   43)?

3. What words did Jesus speak from the cross, according to Matt. 27:46; Mk. 15:34; Lk. 23:34, 46?

4. Notice the allusions to Psalm 22 in the following
   passages: Mk. 15:24 (Ps. 22:18); Mk. 15:29 (Ps. 22:
   7); Matt. 27:43 (Ps. 22:8). According to Matthew
   and Mark, Jesus' last words from the cross were a
   quotation from Psalm 22 (Matt. 27:46; Mk. 15:34;
   Ps. 22:1). How does Psalm 22 end? Do you think
   that Jesus could have had the entire psalm in mind
   when he quoted the first verse?

5. When Jesus died, the synoptic gospels report that
   the curtain of the temple was torn in two, from
   top to bottom (cf. Mk. 15:38). This curtain

separated the main room of the temple from the Holy of Holies, where God was conceived as invisibly enthroned. No one entered the Holy of Holies except the high priest, once a year. What do you think the rending of the curtain symbolized?

6. When Jesus died, Mark reports that the centurion watching Jesus said, "Truly this man was a (the) son of God!" (Mk. 15:39; cf. Matt. 27:54). According to Mark, the centurion was the first person to make this affirmation. Why do you think it is significant that the affirmation comes at this point?

7. Who was responsible for the burial of Jesus, according to Mk. 15:42-47?

8. According to Mk. 14:28 and 16:7, where would Jesus appear after his resurrection? According to some early manuscripts, the original form of Mark ended at 16:8, and thus Mark did not actually record any resurrection appearances. The "Longer Ending" of Mark (16:9-20) may have been added as early as the second century.

9. Where did the risen Lord appear, according to Matt. 28:16-20? What command did he give his disciples?

10. In what area did the risen Lord appear, according to Lk. 24:13-53? How do the accounts in Luke emphasize the reality of the resurrection of Jesus? What are the disciples to do, according to Lk. 24:47?

15. Acts

1. Compare Lk. 1:1-4 with Acts 1:1-5. What indication do these passages give that Luke and Acts were written by the same author? How would you describe the literary style of these passages?

2. Note the following verses in Acts, which serve as summaries of major divisions of the book: 6:7; 9:31; 12:24; 16:5; 19:20; 28:31. From what capital city does the expansion of Christianity begin? To what capital city does Christianity come, at the end of

Acts? Why do you think the author of Acts regarded these two cities as especially significant?

3. In Acts 1:6-8, how does the author deal with a) the problem that the present age had not ended, as the earliest Christians expected; b) the need to define the role of the Christian community after the death and resurrection of Jesus?

4. What was the fate of Judas, according to Acts 1:18? Cf. Matt. 27:3-10. What were the qualifications for the man who was chosen to succeed Judas, according to Acts 1:21-22?

5. What happened at Pentecost, according to Acts 2:1-13? Can you explain why this event is sometimes interpreted as a reversal of the tower of Babel account in Genesis 11:1-9?

6. What themes did Peter present in his Pentecost sermon in Acts 2:14-40? Can these themes also be found in the synoptic gospels? What do you think is the meaning of "all that are far off" in Acts 2:39?

7. How did the early Christians in Jerusalem live and worship in their daily lives, according to Acts 2:42-47; 4:31-35?

8. How did the early Christians explain the fact that the Messiah had suffered and died in accomplishing his work? What was their attitude toward the Jews in this respect? Cf. especially Acts 2:22-24; 3:12-21.

9. What is the meaning of Peter's words in Acts 4:12? On the basis of this verse, how would you understand the relationship between Christianity and other religions?

10. What charges were brought against Stephen, according to Acts 6:8-15? What criticisms of Judaism did Stephen make in his speech in Acts 7?

11. Saul (Paul) is first mentioned in Acts 7:58-8:3. What activities was he engaged in then? How did he become a Christian, according to Acts 9? How did he escape from Damascus? Who introduced him to the apostles in Jerusalem?

12. Who was Cornelius, according to Acts 10:1-11:18? Was he a Jew or a Gentile? What conclusion did Peter come to after visiting Cornelius?

13. What happened in Antioch, according to Acts 11:19-30? What was the role of Barnabas there? What name did the disciples receive there?

14. Paul's first missionary journey is described in Acts 13:1-14:28. Who accompanied Paul? Where did they go? Did they speak to Jews or Gentiles, or both? Would you say that they were successful in their work?

15. Compare Paul's sermon in Antioch of Pisidia (Acts 13:16-41) with Peter's Pentecost sermon (Acts 2:14-40; cf. question 6). Do they make essentially the same points?

16. What issue was discussed at the "Jerusalem Conference" of Acts 15:1-35? Which viewpoint prevailed, according to this account? What would have happened to the early Christian movement if the other side had prevailed?

17. Paul's second missionary journey is described in Acts 15:36-19:20. Who accompanied him on this trip? To what new continent did they carry Christianity?

18. What happened when Paul was in prison in Philippi (Acts 16)? Did the Roman authorities find any valid charge against him?

19. What points did Paul make in his sermon on the Areopagus in Athens, according to Acts 17? How did the Athenians react to the idea of resurrection? Did Paul have much success in Athens?

20. Did Paul have much success in Corinth, according to Acts 18? Who were Aquila and Priscilla? Why had they left Rome? Did Gallio, the proconsul of Achaia, find any valid charge against Paul?

21. Who was Apollos, according to Acts 18:24-28? How did Priscilla and Aquila help him in Ephesus?

22. Paul's third journey is described in Acts 19:21-21:17. Where did he go on this trip?

23. Who was Demetrius? Why did he object to Paul's

preaching in Ephesus, according to Acts 19:23-41?

24. What themes did Paul develop in his farewell speech to the elders of Ephesus, when he asked them to come to him in Miletus (Acts 20:17-38)?

25. When Paul spoke to the Jewish council in Jerusalem, how did he refer to the different beliefs of the Pharisees and the Sadducees (Acts 23:1-10)?

26. When Paul was taken to Caesarea and held in prison (Acts 23:26-26:32), did the political authorities find that he had committed any wrong? Why did he "appeal to Caesar," i.e., ask that his case be tried in Rome?

27. When Paul was taken to Rome, did he find Christians already there (Acts 28)? Is there any indication when they had arrived or who had founded the church there?

28. What did Paul do while he was awaiting trial in Rome (Acts 28)? Why do you think the book of Acts ends without telling the outcome of the trial?

16. I Thessalonians

1. Since I Thessalonians may have been Paul's earliest letter (about A.D. 50 or 51), note the three parts of the address: "Paul... to... grace to you and peace." This form occurs in I and II Thessalonians, Galatians, I and II Corinthians, Romans, Colossians, Philemon, Philippians, and Ephesians. Also, in these letters, the words "grace to you and peace" always occur in the same order. How would you compare this form of address with those in I and II Timothy and Titus?

2. The word "grace" (charis) echoes the usual word of greeting in Greek (chairein); the word "peace" (eirene) reflects the Hebrew word for peace (shalom) which was used as a greeting. How do the words "grace" and "peace" reflect Paul's background? Do they also reflect important themes of his faith?

3. What characteristics of Christian life does Paul

mention in I Thess. 1:2-10, as they are illustrated by the Thessalonians and by Paul himself?

4. Note the words "faith, love, hope" in I Thess. 1:3. How are these related to the other words in these phrases, "work, labor, steadfastness"?

5. How had Paul and his companions acted when they were in Thessalonica, according to I Thess. 2:1-12?

6. What was Timothy's role, according to I Thess. 3:1-10? What good news had he brought? How did Paul react?

7. Note that Paul uses a singular verb ("direct") in his prayer in I Thess. 3:11. What does this suggest about his way of thinking about God and Jesus?

8. To whom should Christian love be shown, according to I Thess. 3:12?

9. What ethical advice does Paul give in I Thess. 4:1-12?

10. In I Thess. 4:13-18, Paul writes about the coming of Jesus and the resurrection of the dead. Does Paul expect this to happen during his lifetime? What special concern on the part of the Thessalonians is he dealing with?

11. What characteristics of Christian life does Paul mention in I Thess. 5:1-22? Can you relate any of these to Jesus' own life and teachings?

12. What do you think is the meaning of the expression "the God of peace" in I Thess. 5:23?

17. II Thessalonians

1. What does Paul give thanks for in II Thess. 1:3-4? Are the Thessalonians still being persecuted (cf. I Thess. 1:6; 2:14)?

2. In II Thess. 1:7b-10, Paul may be quoting from an early Christian hymn. What themes does the passage

express? What do you think is meant by the idea that Jesus will be "glorified in his saints"?

3. In II Thess. 2:1-12, Paul gives a description of events that must take place before the present age of history ends: a) some force or person is now restraining the "man of lawlessness"; b) the man of lawlessness will be revealed; c) Jesus will come and destroy the man of lawlessness. Although the details are obscure, the man of lawlessness is apparently a figure borrowed from Jewish mythology who was expected to appear as a false Messiah. Why do you think Paul wrote this section, in which he stressed that certain events must take place before the present age ends?

4. Several interpretations have been offered for the restraining force or person alluded to in II Thess. 2:6-7: the Roman empire and emperor; the Holy Spirit; the preaching of the Gospel. Can you explain what each of these would mean?

5. Some interpreters have argued that Paul's view of the future in I Thess. 5:1-2 is different from that in II Thess. 2:1-12. Do you think this is true? Explain.

6. In Paul's prayer in II Thess. 2:16-17, note that the verbs in vs. 17 are singular. Cf. I Thess. 3: 11 (Topic 16, question 7).

7. In II Thess. 3:6-15, Paul points out that some of the Thessalonians are not working for a living. The play on words in vs. 11 could be translated as "not busy, but busybodies." Why do you think these people have taken this attitude? What advice does Paul give?

8. What is the meaning of II Thess. 3:17? What does it suggest about the process of writing the letter?

18. Galatians

1. The opening address in the letter to the Galatians
    is 1:1-5; for the basic outline of the address, cf.
    Topic 16, question 1. What themes does Paul
    present in this address, in addition to the basic
    outline? How do these themes suggest the two main
    points that he will emphasize in the letter (i.e.,
    his authority as an apostle, and the principle of
    justification by faith)?

2. After the opening address in Galatians, Paul omits
    the passage of thanksgiving to God that is customary
    in his other letters. Why do you think he omits the
    thanksgiving in this letter?

3. In Gal. 1:11-2:10, how does Paul emphasize a) the
    authenticity of his message and his role as an
    apostle; b) his independence of the Jerusalem
    church; c) his concern for establishing a working
    relationship with the Jerusalem church?

4. Justification, for Paul, probably meant being
    forgiven by God and being reconciled to God.
    According to Gal. 2:15-21, does Paul think that a
    person is justified through faith in Christ or by
    obeying the requirements of the Jewish law? Why?
    In this respect, how would you compare Paul's view
    of justification with Jesus' view of the kingdom
    of God?

5. What is the meaning of the reference to Abraham in
    Gal. 3:6-9? Why do you think Paul chose a figure
    from the Old Testament to illustrate his point?

6. About A.D. 150 an early Christian named Marcion
    issued a version of Galatians that omitted 3:6-9.
    If you are familiar with Marcion's views, can you
    explain why he would want to omit these verses?

7. What does Paul mean by his example of a human will,
    in Gal. 3:15-20? Note that the same Greek word can
    mean "will" or "covenant."

8. According to Gal. 3:21-29, did Paul regard the
    Jewish law as good or bad in itself? What function
    had it served in the past? Why was it superseded
    now? Note that in vss. 24-25, Paul speaks of a

"custodian." In Greek society this was a slave who accompanied a child to school. What does Paul mean by this metaphor?

9. Why does Paul consider it so dangerous to "relapse" into reliance on the law as a way of salvation? Cf. especially Gal. 2:21; 3:10-14; 5:1-6. What is the counterpart for Christians today to such reliance?

10. If Paul believes that a person is justified by faith, does he still think that a person should lead an ethical life and a life of service to others? Cf. especially Gal. 5:13-26. What would Paul say to those people (known as antinomians) who thought that conduct was unimportant because a person was justified by faith?

19. I Corinthians

1. In I Cor. 1:2, Paul addresses the people of Corinth as "saints." Were the Christians in Corinth the kind of people who would usually be called saints? What did Paul mean by the term? Cf. I Cor. 1:30.

2. According to I Cor. 1:10-17; 3:5-9, what factions existed in the church at Corinth? How had they arisen? How did Paul deal with this problem? How did he regard other Christian workers such as Apollos (cf. Acts 18:24-19:1)? Did the divisions in Corinth arise for the same reason as different denominations today?

3. According to I Cor. 1:17-2:5, what themes did Paul emphasize in his preaching? Why was Jesus' death on the cross an obstacle in preaching to Jews and Gentiles? What kind of Messiah did the Jews expect? How did the Gentiles seek knowledge of God?

4. In I Cor. 1:17-2:16, Paul also deals with the theme of wisdom. When he speaks of "a secret and hidden wisdom of God" (2:7), he apparently means God's full plan of salvation as it is revealed in Christ. How does Paul believe people can understand this form of wisdom?

5. Paul also speaks of "the wisdom of the world" (1:20).

What do you think he means by this kind of wisdom? Would he disparage human learning and knowledge in themselves?

6. What does Paul suggest about the membership of the church in Corinth, in I Cor. 1:26-31? What criticism of the Corinthians does he make in I Cor. 4:6-13? Why?

7. What beliefs about Christ does Paul express in I Cor. 1:30; 3:11; 8:6? How would you explain these ideas in present-day language?

8. What characteristics should the Christian community have, according to I Cor. 3:16-17? Note that Paul is thinking in terms of a corporate image in these verses, since the word for "you" is plural. Can you relate this passage to the expectation of a Jewish writing (I Enoch 91:13) that in the new age God would build a new temple to dwell in?

9. In I Cor. 6:12, Paul quotes a slogan that was popular among some Christians in Corinth: "All things are lawful for me." How did this slogan represent a misunderstanding of Paul's principle of justification by faith? In what two ways does Paul qualify this idea? Which qualification refers to individual life? Which one refers to the life of the community? (Cf. also Topic 18, question 10.)

10. In I Cor. 7, Paul discusses the topic of marriage, noting that marriage is not wrong in itself but advising that it is preferable not to marry. What two reasons does he give for this advice?

11. What attitude does Paul express toward slavery, in I Cor. 7:20-24? Why do you think he has this view?

12. In I Cor. 10:1-5, Paul refers to several events at the time of Moses: crossing the sea out of Egypt, eating manna and quail, and drinking water that flowed from a rock. (He also reflects a rabbinic tradition that the same rock followed the Israelites during their wilderness wanderings.) Paul regards these events as "types" or models of the Christian sacraments of baptism and the Lord's Supper. In making this comparison, what did he want to indicate to the Corinthians?

13. In I Cor. 10:14-22; 11:23-26, Paul discusses the

meaning of the Lord's Supper. Which aspects refer to the past, the present, and the future? Which aspects does Paul emphasize?

14. The Lord's Supper at this time was a regular meal, presumably in a private home. According to I Cor. 11:17-22, 33-34, what problems arose when the Corinthians celebrated the Lord's Supper? Do you think these problems could have been related to the one discussed in question 2? How does Paul deal with these issues? What is the significance of Paul's view for today?

15. As Paul describes Christian love (agape) in I Cor. 13, how is it related to spiritual gifts such as speaking in tongues, prophecy, knowledge, and faith? How does Christian love treat other people? How would you compare Paul's view of Christian love with Jesus' own life and teachings?

16. According to I Cor. 15, what connection does Paul find between the resurrection of Christ and the resurrection of Christians? How does his view of the "spiritual body" differ from a) the Greek idea of an immortal soul, and b) the view of resurrection in some Jewish sources as the restoration of the physical body? At this point in his life, does Paul expect the resurrection to occur soon?

20. II Corinthians

1. According to some interpreters, chapters 10-13 in II Corinthians were originally part of a "stern letter" that Paul wrote to Corinth when the Christians there rebelled against his authority. Some other Christian leaders with a strong Jewish background had apparently come to Corinth and sought to undermine Paul's authority. What does Paul say about these people, and how does he compare himself with them, in II Cor. 11:4-6, 22-23?

2. Had Paul accepted support from the Corinthians when he worked among them, according to II Cor. 11:7-11?

3. What kind of hardships had Paul suffered in his work, according to II Cor. 11:23-29? Why do you

think he mentions these?

4. Had Paul or his helpers taken any advantage of the Corinthians when they were with them, according to II Cor. 12:14-18? Why do you think Paul raises this point?

5. What does Paul fear he may find when he visits Corinth again, according to II Cor. 12:19-21? Had he dealt with such issues in I Corinthians?

6. II Cor. 1-9 may represent a "thankful letter" that Paul wrote after he learned that his "stern letter" had convinced the Corinthians to acknowledge the validity of his work among them. What feelings does he reflect in II Cor. 1:3-7? Note that the word "comfort," as a noun or a verb, occurs ten times in this passage. It has the connotations of encouragement and strength as well as consolation.

7. What does II Cor. 1:20 suggest about the relationship between the Old Testament and Christianity? How would you compare this with Gal. 3:6-9?

8. A certain Christian in Corinth had been especially critical of Paul. How does Paul want the Corinthians to treat this person now, according to II Cor. 2:5-11?

9. What characteristics of Christian leadership does Paul describe in II Cor. 1:12, 24; 2:17; 3:4-6; 4:1-2, 5?

10. What aspects of life after death does Paul describe briefly in II Cor. 4:14?

11. In II Cor. 5:1-9, Paul also discusses life after death. What metaphors does he use here which correspond to the idea of the "spiritual body" in I Cor. 15?

12. Note that Paul speaks of judgment in II Cor. 5:10. If he believes that salvation is a gift of God's grace, how can he speak of judgment? Explain.

13. What do you think Paul means by a "new creation" in II Cor. 5:17? How does he explain this idea in the following verses? Does it mean that he no longer has any expectations for the future? Cf. the

similar imagery in II Cor. 4:6.

14. Paul's helper, Titus, had carried the "stern letter" to Corinth and had then gone to Macedonia. When Paul met him in Macedonia, what news did he bring about the Corinthians (II Cor. 7:5-16)?

15. In I Cor. 16:1-4, Paul had discussed a financial contribution for the church in Jerusalem. He returns to this topic in II Cor. 8:1-7, using the churches of Macedonia as an example. Note that the word charis is used three ways in this passage: the "grace" of God (8:1), the "favor" of sharing in the contribution (8:4), and the "gracious work" of the contribution itself (8:6, 7). What do these meanings of the word suggest about the meaning of Christian stewardship?

16. In II Cor. 8:8-15, what do you think Paul means when he describes Christ as "rich" and "poor"? In what context does he make these references to Christ?

21. Romans

1. In the opening address (Rom. 1:1-7), notice that Paul uses the word "called" three times. What does he wish to indicate by using this word? Since the Christians in Rome may have been of a conservative Jewish background, Paul may have felt the need to correct doubts about his role as an apostle and his mission to the Gentiles.

2. In Rom. 1:8-17 and 15:14-33, how does Paul make a special effort to be tactful in writing to the Christians in Rome? Why does he do this? Why had he not visited them before? Where does he plan to go after seeing them? Why do you think he emphasizes that Christianity is a universal faith, intended for Gentiles as well as Jews?

3. In Rom. 1:17, Paul speaks of the "righteousness" of God. Is this simply an attribute of God, or is it also an act of God on behalf of men? In answering this question, try to determine how the Hebrew word for righteousness (tsedaqah) is used in Isaiah

46:13; 51:6; and Psalm 24:5.

4. In Rom. 1:18-3:20, Paul discusses the situation of
    mankind apart from Christ. He treats the Gentiles
    first and then the Jews; together they represent
    all mankind. What knowledge of God do the Gentiles
    have (cf. especially 1:19-23; 2:14-16)? Do they
    live according to this knowledge? What knowledge
    of God do the Jews have (cf. especially 2:17-24)?
    Do they live according to this knowledge?

5. In Rom. 3:21-4:25, Paul discusses the principle of
    justification by faith. How is this section
    related to the preceding section (1:18-3:20)? Does
    a person earn justification, or is it a gift of
    God's grace? Does justification by faith apply to
    Jews alone, or to Gentiles also?

6. In chapters 5-8 of Romans, Paul describes the new
    life that is available to the Christian. How does
    God show his love, according to Rom. 5:8? What is
    the meaning of Christ's death, according to Rom.
    5:9-11? Who is reconciled to whom, according to
    this passage? Who takes the initiative in bringing
    about reconciliation? Is reconciliation the same
    idea as justification? From what should the Christ-
    ian be free, according to Rom. 6:2? From what is
    the Christian free, according to Rom. 7:6? From
    what is the Christian free, according to Rom. 8:11?

7. What is Paul's attitude toward the Jews in chapters
    9-11 of Romans? What roles do Jews and Gentiles
    have in God's purposes for human history? What is
    God's ultimate wish for all mankind?

8. Compare Paul's ethical teachings in chapters 12-14
    of Romans with Jesus' life and teachings in the
    synoptic gospels. Cf. especially Rom. 12:2, 10,
    14, 16-18; 13:7-9; 14:13, 19.

9. Notice how Paul develops his thought in the main
    sections of Romans that are indicated above in
    questions 4, 5, 6, and 8. How would you state these
    ideas in terms that apply to the world today?

10. In Rom. 1:5, Paul speaks of "obedience to the faith."
    The Greek words are literally "obedience of faith."
    They could mean obedience to Christ which comes from
    faith. What is the difference between the two

interpretations? Which do you think is correct?

11. Paul's statement in Rom. 3:23, pantes hemarton,
can be interpreted as "all sin" (gnomic aorist) or
"all have sinned" (cumulative aorist). The first
is a general statement about human nature; the
second is a summary statement about men's actions
in the course of history. Which do you think is
correct? Why?

12. In Rom. 3:24, Paul speaks of being "justified."
This could refer to a) actual righteousness (God
acknowledges the righteousness of the believer);
b) imputed righteousness (God declares the believer
to be righteous, even though he is not); c) imparted
righteousness (God makes the believer to be righteous); d) forgiveness and reconciliation (God forgives the believer and brings him into the right
relation with himself). Note that the first three
meanings imply that God requires some kind of
righteousness on the part of the believer, while the
fourth meaning does not make this condition. Which
meaning of justification do you think is correct?
Cf. especially Rom. 5:6-11.

13. In Rom. 3:25, Paul speaks of the death of Christ as
hilasterion. Sometimes this is translated as
"propitiation" (appeasing an angry deity) and
sometimes as "expiation" (removing sin and estab-
lishing forgiveness). Which do you think is
correct? Why? Note that in the Greek translation
of the Old Testament this word was used for the
"mercy seat," the lid of the ark above which God
was invisibly enthroned.

14. In Rom. 6:1, Paul refers to the antinomian objection
that ethical living is not important because
justification is by faith rather than works. Note
that he uses three illustrations in 6:2-7:6 -
baptism, slavery, and marriage. Is he making the
same point in all three, or not?

15. What confidence regarding the future does Paul have,
according to Rom. 8:31-39? Why do you think he
speaks of both the love of Christ (vs. 35) and the
love of God (vs. 39)? Is he referring to the love
that God and Christ show to people, or the love that
people have for them?

16. Rom. 13:1-7 is the only passage in which Paul deals

at length with the Christian view of the state. How would you compare this passage with Mk. 12:13-17? Do you think Paul meant that a Christian should approve of everything that a government does?

17. Notice that Paul refers to the Ten Commandments in Rom. 13:9. Does he think that Christians should still obey these commandments? How are they related to the principle of love for neighbor?

18. In Rom. 15:26, Paul refers to the collection that he is raising in Macedonia and Greece for the Christians in Jerusalem. He speaks of this collection here as a koinonia, a term that usually means sharing or fellowship. What does this term suggest about the purpose of the collection?

22. Colossians

1. Where was Paul when he wrote to the Colossians, according to Col. 4:2-18? What helpers were with him or in touch with him? Which of these people were from Colossae?

2. Had Paul ever been in Colossae? Cf. Col. 1:4; 2:1. Who apparently had founded the church there, according to Col. 1:5-7?

3. Paul wrote to the Colossians because a gnostic-like religious philosophy had become popular in Colossae. Apparently it was not specifically Christian, but it was willing to find a place for Christ as one of the subordinate divine beings in the universe. This movement emphasized the worship of certain angelic beings (Col. 2:18), called "the elemental spirits of the universe" (Col. 2:8), and organized into ranks, with titles (cf. Col. 1:16). What does Paul think of this movement, according to Col. 2:4, 8?

4. The religious philosophy at Colossae apparently held that a person must learn about all the spiritual beings or powers in the universe in order to know the "totality" or "fullness" of divine reality. How does Paul challenge this view in Col. 1:19; 2:9? If Christ were only one of many spiritual beings in the

universe, what would be the meaning of God's revelation of himself through Christ?

5. How many times does Paul use the word "all" in Col. 1:15-20? Why does he emphasize this word? How does he describe Christ in this passage? Does Paul think that there can be a higher type of religious experience than worshiping God as he has made himself known in Christ?

6. The idea popular in Colossae - that a person must worship Christ and other spiritual beings - is somewhat comparable to the position of a person today who gives his loyalty to Christ and other causes or "ism's." Can you think of examples of such "ism's"? Can these have some value in themselves? How can a person know how much importance to give them?

7. In several passages Paul also refers to other aspects of the religious philosophy popular at Colossae: a Jewish type of legalism concerning food, drink, and festivals (Col. 2:16), an emphasis on "visions" (Col. 2:18), and a tendency toward asceticism (Col. 2:18, 20-23). What does Paul think of these beliefs and practices?

8. What prayers or hopes does Paul express with regard to the Colossians, in Col. 1:9-12, 23, 28; 2:1-7?

9. Note that Paul uses past tenses in Col. 1:13 ("delivered... transferred") to emphasize what God has already done for Christians. Why do you think he emphasizes this in writing to the Colossians?

10. In Col. 1:27; 3:1-4, Paul refers to the Christian hope for the future. What is the basis for this hope? What (implicitly) is not necessary?

11. The expression "his beloved Son" in Col. 1:13 is literally "the Son of his love." It may mean the Son whom God loves, or the Son who is the perfect embodiment of God's love for the world. Which do you think it means? Are both meanings possible?

12. In Col. 3:5-17, Paul describes the transformation of the Christian, in character and conduct, as the "new man" is continually "being renewed." Does Paul speak of attitudes, or actions, or both? Is he

thinking of the individual person, the Christian
community, or both?

13. In Col. 3:18-4:1, Paul gives a "table of household
duties," describing how various members of the
household should act toward one another. What kind
of family structure does Paul presuppose? What
effect would his advice have in terms of that
structure? How is his advice significant today?

23. Philemon

1. Where was Paul when he wrote his letter to Philemon,
according to Philem. 1, 9, 13?

2. Paul had apparently met Onesimus, a run-away slave,
in prison, and had introduced him to Christianity.
What information does he give about Onesimus in Col.
4:9? Does he want to send him back, according to
Philem. 11-14? Why is he doing so?

3. The name Onesimus means "useful" or "beneficial."
How does Paul allude to this meaning in Philem. 11,
20?

4. In Philem. 9, Paul refers to himself as an "old man"
(presbytes) or an "ambassador" (presbeutes). The
first reading has better support in early manuscripts, but some translators prefer the second.
Which reading do you think is supported by the
context?

5. Philemon, as a slave owner, had the power or punish-
ing or even executing a run-away slave. What does
Paul ask Philemon to do, according to Philem. 15-18?
Does he ask Philemon to set Onesimus free?

6. In his commentary on Philemon in The Interpreter's
Bible, Vol. 11 (New York and Nashville: Abingdon
Press, 1955, especially pp. 556-560), John Knox
advocates the theory that Paul's purpose in writing
the letter was not to persuade the owner to receive
Onesimus back without inflicting severe penalties,
but to ask the owner to send Onesimus back to Paul
so that he could continue to assist Paul. (Knox
further believes that Onesimus later became bishop

106

of the church at Ephesus and supervised the collection of Paul's letters there.) Knox's arguments
include the following: in converting Onesimus to
Christianity, Paul had made him genuinely "useful"
(vss. 10-11); Paul wanted Onesimus to serve him as
an assistant (vs. 12); as the owner's "partner"
(vs. 17; a business term), Paul had a right to
share the owner's possessions; Paul offered to
assume Onesimus' debts after he was freed (vs. 18);
Paul was confident that the owner would grant "even
more" than he explicitly asked for (vs. 21).   In
light of your study of the letter, what do you
think was Paul's purpose?

24. Philippians

1. Where was Paul when he wrote this letter, according
to Philip. 1:7, 13, 17? What had the Philippians
sent to Paul, according to Philip. 4:18? Whom had
they sent to assist him, according to Philip. 2:25-
30? Why is Paul sending him back to Philippi?

2. What do you think is the meaning of the expressions
"first day" and "the beginning of the gospel," in
Philip. 1:5 and 4:15? Cf. Acts 16:9-12.

3. Has Paul enjoyed good relationships with the
Christians in Philippi, according to Philip. 1:3-11?
How does he tactfully suggest that they may still
need to grow in living Christian lives?

4. In Philip. 1:19-26, Paul discusses the topics of
life and death. What values does he see in each,
within the context of his Christian faith?

5. What is the main theme of Paul's advice in Philip.
2:1-4?

6. What is the main theme of Paul's reference to Christ
in Philip. 2:5-11? How is it related to the advice
that he has just given (question 5)?

7. The "hymn to Christ" in Philip. 2:5-11 is carefully
written in balanced phrases. Some interpreters
think that Paul is quoting here from an early
Christian hymn or poem; others think that Paul

wrote the passage himself. What periods or phases of Christ's existence does the passage describe? What do you think is the meaning of "emptied himself" in vs. 7? Does it mean that Christ gave up his divine nature, certain attributes of divinity, or certain privileges of his previous status? What is the "name" that Christ received, according to vss. 9–11?

8. In Philip. 2:15, Paul expresses the hope that the Christians in Philippi may shine as "lights." He uses a Greek word that is always applied to the heavenly bodies. Why do you think he chooses this word?

9. In Philip. 3:4–11, Paul summarizes his credentials and accomplishments in Judaism. Are these important to him now? What does he regard as important?

10. What phrase from I Cor. 15 does Paul apparently refer to in Philip. 3:21?

11. Philip. 4:8 gives a list of virtues admired in the non–Christian world? What attitude does Paul take toward the best of non–Christian thought?

12. In Philip. 4:11, Paul writes that he has learned to be "content" under any circumstances. He uses a Stoic term (autarkes) that means literally "self-sufficient." How does Paul give new meaning to the term in vs. 13?

25. Ephesians

1. Some interpreters believe that Ephesians was written by a follower of Paul, about a generation after his death, as a general letter addressed to all Christians. Note that the phrase "at Ephesus" (1:1) is placed in the footnotes of the Revised Standard Version; it is missing from the earliest manuscripts (the Chester Beatty papyrus of the third century, and Codex Vaticanus and Codex Sinaiticus of the fourth century). Is there any other reference to Ephesus in the letter?

2. Is the writer personally acquainted with the recipi-

ents, according to Eph. 1:15; 3:2? Compare Acts 20:31. Does the writer refer to specific persons or problems?

3. The thanksgiving (Eph. 1:3-14) focuses on God's work of salvation in Christ. At what point did God decide upon his plan of salvation? What words describe God's attitude and actions toward people? What words describe the gifts or benefits that people receive through Christ? Is there any indication that all parts of the universe share in salvation, in a manner that is appropriate to them?

4. In what ways did God exhibit his "great might," according to Eph. 1:15-23? What do you think the writer means by describing the church as the "body" and the "fullness" of Christ (vs. 23)?

5. In what sense does the writer believe that Christians have already experienced "resurrection," according to Eph. 2:1-10? Have they been saved by God's grace or their own good works? Are "works" important? Why?

6. In Eph. 2:11-22, the writer discusses the spiritual unity of mankind in Christ. Note that the expression "far off" in vss. 13 and 17 apparently reflects a rabbinic way of referring to Gentiles. What was the former spiritual situation of Gentiles? What is their present situation as believers in Christ? How do you think this spiritual unity of Jews and Gentiles is related to the idea of unity in Eph. 1:10?

7. In Eph. 3:1-13, the writer discusses his own mission and message. What do you think he means by "mystery" in vss. 4-6? How does he describe the purpose of the church in vs. 10?

8. Summarize some of the ways in which the writer describes the Christian life in Eph. 3:14-6:20. What aspects does the writer stress? In what ways does he refer to Christ as the source of Christian life or an example for Christian life?

9. Which other letter most closely resembles Ephesians? List some examples of similar phrases or passages.

26. The Gospel of John

1. In the Prologue to John (1:1-18), what is meant by the Word (Logos)? What is the relation of the Word to creation? to the Jews? to the law? to Christians? to Jesus? to God? to revelation?

2. Compare John's statements about the Word with Gen. 1:1; Ps. 33:6-9; Prov. 8:22-31; Is. 55:11; Col. 1:15-17.

3. It is sometimes suggested today that Christianity should give up its traditional language about God, Christ, etc., and restate its message in modern terms. How would you restate the themes of the Prologue in this way?

4. Why do you think it was important to John that "the Word became flesh" (1:14)? What view was he probably combatting here?

5. What does John mean by the "world" in 1:10? in 3:16-17? Can the term still have these meanings today?

6. Compare John 1:24-34 with Mark's account of the baptism of Jesus (Mk. 1:9-11). Is there any difference? Why?

7. What symbolism was involved when Jesus changed water into wine, according to John 2:1-11? What was the purpose of Jesus' signs, according to 2:11? How is the word "signs" used in the synoptic gospels?

8. The expression "kingdom of God" occurs in John only in 3:3, 5. Is it present or future here? How does this compare with synoptic usage? What does it mean to Christians today to think of the kingdom as present? as future?

9. According to 3:1-15, whom was Jesus addressing when he spoke of the need to be born again? What sacrament is suggested by the reference to water? Is water or spirit more important in this passage? Note that the same Greek word can mean "wind" or "spirit." How does John use this double meaning?

10. How are men judged, according to 3:16-21? When?
    How does this compare with the view of judgment in
    the synoptics?

11. Is everlasting life present or future, according to
    3:36; 5:24; 6:47? How does this compare with the
    view of the synoptics?

12. Compare 5:26 with 5:30. If the Son has life in
    himself, why can he do nothing on his own authority?
    See also 7:18.

13. Compare Mark 6:30-44 with John 6:1-15, 25-40. Is
    Jesus' part the same in each account? What do you
    think the bread signifies in each account?

14. What do you think is the meaning of the ideas of
    truth and freedom, according to 8:31-38? In Jewish
    thought, truth was the Law, and study of the Law
    made a person free.

15. In John 9, what do you think the healing of the
    blind man symbolizes? What view of suffering is
    expressed? Does Jesus accept this explanation?
    What are the different reactions to the healing?
    Who does Jesus think is really blind? Why?

16. In 10:1-18, note the three groups of sheep: the
    shepherd's own sheep within the sheepfold (vss. 3-
    4), other sheep within the fold (implied by vss. 3-
    4), and other sheep not of the fold (vs. 16). What
    people does each group symbolize? What does the
    shepherd do for the sheep? Is this theme present
    in Luke 15:3-7?

17. In John 12:20-26, why is it significant that some
    Greeks appear? Have they appeared before? Why do
    they speak to Philip? What does Jesus mean by the
    "hour"? Compare 2:4; 7:30; 8:20. What does Jesus
    mean by being "glorified"?

18. What was the purpose of the foot-washing in John 13?
    Who usually did this for guests? Why do you think
    John has this incident instead of the words explain-
    ing the bread and the wine, as in the synoptics?

19. What is the meaning of the "new commandment" that
    Jesus gives in 13:34-35? How is this different from
    the "two great commandments" of Mark 12:28-34?

20. How does one know the Father, according to 14:1-11?

21. What is the function of the Holy Spirit, according to 14:26? Note that most texts have the reading, "all things that I said to you." A few ancient texts read, "whatever I say to you." Is there any difference?

22. Who is the vine in Ps. 80:8-11; Is. 5:1-7? Who is the vine in Mk. 12:1-12? Who is the vine in John 15? How do you think John is reinterpreting earlier tradition?

23. In John 17, does Jesus pray for anything for himself? For whom else does he pray? What does he ask for them? Why do Jesus' followers engage in mission to the world?

24. Compare John 19:17 with Mark 15:21. Why might John stress that Jesus carried his own cross?

25. When do the disciples receive the Holy Spirit, according to John 20:22? Compare with Acts 1:8; 2:1-4. What does this event signify to each writer?

26. It is often said that the synoptic gospels tell the story of Jesus' life, and the gospel of John is a meditation on the meaning of his life. Evaluate critically both parts of this statement. To what extent is the writer of John interested in revelation through historical events?

27. How would you explain the following remark by Clement of Alexandria (died A.D. 220)? "... last of all, John, perceiving that the external facts had been made plain in the gospel, being urged by friends, and inspired by the Spirit, composed a spiritual gospel."

27. I, II, and III John

1. What aspects of Christian life does the author of I John refer to in 1:5-10; 2:1-11; 3:4-10, 19-24?

2. Some early Christians, known as docetists, thought that Jesus only "seemed" to be human and to undergo

the experiences of suffering and death. What does the writer of I John think of this view, according to 4:1-3?

3. Analyze the discussion of Christian love in I John 4:7-21. Of what three relationships does the writer use the word? Which form of love is basic to the others? How did God make known his love for people?

4. On the basis of questions 1-3, how would you summarize the writer's understanding of the distinguishing characteristics of a Christian?

5. An important idea in I John is that the believer "abides" in God and God "abides" in the believer. Under what conditions does this occur, according to 3:24; 4:15; 4:16? How would you compare these conditions with your summary in question 4?

6. How does the writer of I John regard the "world," according to 2:15-17; 5:19? How would you compare this attitude with that in the gospel of John (Topic 26, question 5)?

7. Does the writer of I John regard everlasting life as a present reality for the Christian, according to 2:17; 3:14; 5:11-13? How would you compare this view with that of the gospel of John (Topic 26, question 11)?

8. What expectations for the future does the writer of I John have, according to 3:1-3; 4:17-18?

9. II John is written to a church and its members (addressed as "the elect lady and her children"). What ideas in vss. 4-6 remind you of I John? What does the author of II John mean by "the deceiver and the antichrist" in vs. 7? How does he think the church members should treat such a person?

10. III John is directed against a certain Diotrephes, who has apparently established himself as the sole leader in the church (perhaps in Ephesus). How was the church in Ephesus governed in Paul's day, according to Acts 20:17? What does the author of III John think of the new situation, in which one person assumes control?

28.   Revelation

1.   The preface (1:1-3) and the prologue (1:4-20).
Where is John when he writes? Why? How does he
describe himself? On what day of the week is he
writing? How would you explain the phrases "what
must soon take place" and "blessed is he who reads
aloud the words of the prophecy"?

2.   Letters to the seven churches (2:1-3:22). Are the
letters arranged in any geographical order? Do
they give any indication that the people in the
churches are now suffering persecution?

3.   What practices or attitudes do the letters condemn?
What virtues do they encourage? What promise do
they make?

4.   The "heavenly prologue" (4:1-5:14). In what sense
is this vision of heaven the real beginning of the
book? Why was it important to the writer to begin
this way? In what ways does the vision of the
throne recall the revelation at Mt. Sinai (cf. Ex.
19:16; 24:10)? Who are the four living creatures
(cf. Is. 6:2-3)? Who are the 24 elders? How can
a "sea" be in heaven (cf. Gen. 1:7)?

5.   How can Jesus be described as both lion and lamb?
What do these words signify? What does the scroll
symbolize? Why can Jesus alone open the scroll?
What view of the world is reflected in 5:3, 13?
Who are the true kings and priests on earth (5:10;
cf. Ex. 19:6)? What verses in chs. 4 and 5 may
reflect early Christian worship?

6.   The Roman emperor Domitian (A.D. 81-96) demanded
that he be addressed as "Lord and God." In light
of this, how would you explain the meaning of 4:11?

7.   What do the four horsemen symbolize (6:2-8)?

8.   Who are the 144,000 in 7:4? (They are probably the
same as the "great multitude" of 7:9, but note how
this extends the concept.) What do the white robes
represent (7:9; cf. 3:5; 6:9-11)?

9.   What does the "woman" symbolize in ch. 12? Who is
her "child"? Who is the "dragon"? Why do events

in this chapter begin in heaven and end on earth?

10. Who is the first "beast" in ch. 13? What is its relation to the dragon of ch. 12? Who is the second "beast" in ch. 13? What does each beast do? What attitude toward the Roman empire is reflected in this chapter?

11. Compare the view of the Roman empire in ch. 13 with Mk. 12:13-17; Rom. 13:1-7; I Pet. 2:13-17. On the basis of these varying views, how would you explain the meaning of Christian citizenship today?

12. What events does the writer expect during and after the thousand-year reign of Christ (ch. 20)?

13. The new Jerusalem (21:1-22:5). Why would the sea be abolished (21:1)? Where will the new Jerusalem be located? Why does the writer use a city to symbolize everlasting life? What are the twelve gates and the twelve foundations? Why does the new Jerusalem have no temple?

14. Compare the ideas and style of the Gospel of John and the book of Revelation. Which regards ever-lasting life as a present reality for the believer? Which looks forward to the gift of everlasting life in the future? Which thinks of judgment primarily as an on-going process in the present? Which thinks of judgment as a future event? Which re-flects a situation of persecution? Which uses a "code language" to convey its meaning? Which uses more abstract terminology, such as light, life, truth?

29. James

1. Compare this writing with a typical letter of Paul, which is addressed to a particular church, deals with problems in that church, includes greetings to specific persons, and closes with a benediction. Does James have these features? How would you describe its literary form?

2. James is addressed to "the twelve tribes in the dispersion" (1:1). This address may refer to

Jewish-Christian communities scattered throughout the Roman empire, or to Christians generally as they live in a hostile world. How does the idea of twelve tribes recall the patriarch Jacob (of which "James" is the English equivalent)?

3. In 1:2-4, 12-15, the author discusses various kinds of "trials." Does he believe that these have any value? How does he reply to the argument that temptation can come from God? Do you think that he may be trying to correct a possible misunderstanding of the Lord's Prayer?

4. In 1:5-8; 3:13-18, the author discusses "wisdom," by which he apparently means the ability to assess the values of life from God's standpoint. How does one receive wisdom? What are its characteristics?

5. What attitude does the writer of James have toward the rich, according to 1:9-11; 2:1-7; 5:1-6? Does he think that the rich should receive special honor in the church? Does he criticize wealth in itself or the methods by which it is obtained?

6. Compare Paul's principle that "a man is justified by faith apart from works of law" (Rom. 3:28) with the statement in James that "a man is justified by works and not by faith alone" (2:24). By "works," Paul meant carrying out the requirements of the Jewish law as a way to receive justification, and James meant expressing faith in concrete acts of helpfulness to others. Is there any inconsistency between the two statements above? Explain.

7. Some Christians, known as antinomians, understood Paul's principle of justification by faith to mean that ethical living and acts of service to others were not necessary. Note the emphasis on "works" in James, 1:22-25 and 2:14-26. Do you think James is opposing Paul or the antinomian misunderstanding of Paul?

8. What does the author of James say about true religion (1:26-27), speech (3:6-12), wars (4:1-3), the brevity of life (4:13-16)?

9. Some interpreters believe that James was written by a Christian teacher around the end of the first century. Others attribute the writing to James the

brother of Jesus, who was killed about A.D. 62.
What do the following New Testament references
indicate about James the brother of Jesus: Mk. 6:1-
6; I Cor. 15:7; Gal. 1:18-19; 2:9-10; Acts 1:14;
15:12-31?

30. Hebrews

1. The main purpose of the author of Hebrews was
    apparently to strengthen the faith of his readers
    so that they could resist persecutions which were
    threatening them. In 10:32-39, he refers to a
    previous persecution, perhaps the one under Nero in
    A.D. 64. How had the Christians acted then?   In
    2:1-4; 6:1-12; 10:19-31; 12:1-29, he advises his
    readers how to act in their present situation,
    perhaps about A.D. 90. What especially does he
    warn against? Have the readers yet faced martyrdom?
    Is this a possibility?

2. In the prologue, 1:1-4, the writer introduces a
    number of themes that are central to his argument.
    How does he describe the relation of Jesus to the
    Old Testament prophets, angels, creation, God?
    What work did Jesus accomplish?

3. In a number of passages the writer describes the
    nature and work of Jesus: 2:9-18; 4:14-16; 5:7-10;
    7:14, 23-28; 9:11-14; 12:2. Why did Jesus have a
    human nature? Why did he suffer? What does he
    continue to do in heaven?

4. Jewish thought held that the Old Testament law had
    been transmitted by angels (Heb. 2:2; cf. Gal. 3:
    19). Note how the author of Hebrews compares Jesus
    to angels in 1:5-2:18. Which is superior to the
    other? What conclusion does the author draw from
    this comparison?

5. In 3:1-6, the author compares Jesus to Moses, the
    founder of Israel as the "house" or "household" of
    God. Does he give a positive or a negative
    estimate of Moses? How does he compare Jesus with
    Moses?

6. In 3:7-4:13, the author refers to the Israelites at

117

the time of Moses, who were unable, because of their disobedience, to enter the land of Canaan and find "rest." How does he transfer this idea of "rest" to his own day?

7. In 6:13-10:31, the author compares Jesus to the Levitical priests in Judaism. He regards Jesus as superior to the Jewish priests because Jesus was "after the order of Melchizedek," who received tithes from Abraham, the forefather of the Jewish priests. In what other ways does he contrast Jesus with the Jewish priests? Note especially the place where sacrifice is offered, the nature of the sacrifice itself, the effect of the sacrifice, and the need for repetition.

8. In 8:6-13; 9:15-22, the writer also speaks of Jesus as the mediator of a new covenant. From what Old Testament book does he quote a passage which looks forward to a new covenant? The word "covenant" in Greek can also mean a "will." What point does the author make on the basis of these two meanings?

9. In 11:1-40, the author gives a list of heroes of faith in the Old Testament. What does he mean by faith? Why do you think he gives this list?

10. In what ways do you think Hebrews has continuing significance for Christians today?

31. I Peter

1. Note, in 1:1, the five provinces in Asia Minor to which the letter was sent. Possibly the writer intended his letter not simply for Christians in these areas but for all Christians who were subject to persecution for their faith. According to 5:13, the letter was sent from "Babylon." On the basis of Rev. 17:9, 18; 18:2-3, what do you think "Babylon" means?

2. A number of passages in I Peter may refer to the rite of baptism: 1:3-5, 22-23; 2:2; 3:18-22. What metaphor does the writer use to describe baptism? How should baptized Christians live? What hopes do they have for the future?

3. What does the writer mean by describing Jesus as the "living stone" in 2:4-10? Compare I Cor. 3:16-17. What parallels do you find between the author's description of Jesus in 2:21-25 and Isaiah 53?

4. In a number of passages the writer speaks of the suffering that his readers may face because of persecution: 1:6-9; 2:19-25; 3:13-4:2; 4:12-19; 5:6-11. How does he urge them to act in this situation? What example does he refer to? When he mentions "God's will" in 3:17 and 4:19, does he mean that God causes suffering or that God wants Christians to be faithful in times of persecution?

5. In 1:1, 17; 2:11, the writer speaks of "exiles" and "exile." What do you think he means by these terms? Cf. Philip. 3:20-21.

6. What do Christians look forward to, according to 1:3-5, 13; 4:7, 13; 5:4? Why do you think the writer mentions these hopes for the future?

7. How does the author of I Peter advise Christians to behave toward the government, in 2:13-17? Is this the same kind of advice that Paul gave in Rom. 13:1-7? Note that I Peter was sent to the province of Asia, to which the book of Revelation was also addressed. Do you think that the author of I Peter was trying to counteract the view of the government in Revelation? Why?

8. What advice does the writer give to servants, wives, and husbands in 2:18-3:7? What reason does he give in each instance? Note that 3:1-6 reflects a situation in which a Christian woman is married to a non-Christian man. Judaism assumed that a wife would share the religion of her husband, but Christianity allowed women independence in religion. In light of this practice, why do you think the writer gives this particular advice to women?

9. What advice does the writer give to elders in the church, in 5:1-11?

32. I Timothy

1. I Timothy, II Timothy, and Titus are often known as "pastoral" letters because they were written from one church leader to other church leaders. What personal qualities should Timothy cultivate, and what activities should he engage in, according to I Tim. 1:3-5, 18-19; 4:6-16; 6:11-16, 20? To what extent do these correspond to the qualifications and functions expected of church leaders today?

2. Note the writer's account of his own experience in 1:12-17. Why does he use himself as an example?

3. For whom should Christians pray, according to 2:1-7? Does God desire all people to be saved? Was Jesus' death on the cross intended to benefit all people? Cf. 4:10.

4. What are the qualifications for the office of bishop, according to 3:1-7? Why do you think there is so much emphasis on personal character and conduct?

5. Are the qualifications for deacons similar to those for bishops, according to 3:8-13? Note the reference to women in the middle of this passage (vs. 11); it is uncertain whether these women are deaconesses or wives of deacons.

6. The "widows" of 5:3-16 may be a special group, supported by the church. How does the writer try to avoid unnecessary burdens for the church?

7. How should elders be treated, according to 5:17-22? Note that this passage does not give special qualifications for elders, but only describes how they should be treated. For this reason it is possible that the elders did not form a separate group from the bishops (literally "superintendents" or "overseers").

8. What does the writer advise about the medicinal use of wine, in 5:23?

9. Compare I Tim. 6:1-2 with Col. 3:22-25. Do they give the same advice to slaves? Does either

suggest changing the institution of slavery? Why?

10. What advice does the writer give about the desire for wealth and the use of wealth (6:17-19)? Why do you think he deals with these topics?

11. Throughout the letter the writer refers occasionally to a "different doctrine" that some are seeking to promote. What are the characteristics of this teaching, according to 1:4, 6-7; 4:1-3, 7; 6:3-5, 20-21? Could it be a gnostic type of teaching? How is Timothy to deal with it?

33.   II Timothy

1. What ideas does the writer mention when he gives thanks to God, in 1:3-7?

2. What charge does the writer give Timothy in 1:8-14? How does he understand the eternal purpose of God toward mankind?

3. In his advice to Timothy in 2:1-7, the writer uses three metaphors (the soldier, the athlete, the farmer). What is the point of each metaphor?

4. What further advice does the author give to Timothy in 2:15, 24-25; 3:14-15; 4:1-5?

5. What do you think the writer means by "scripture" in 3:14-17? What values does he find in scripture?

6. In 2:11-13, the writer may be quoting from an early baptismal liturgy. What would these verses mean to newly baptized Christians?

7. In 2:17-18, the author refers to Hymenaeus and Philetus, who held that the resurrection was already past. Hymenaeus is mentioned elsewhere only in I Tim. 1:20; Philetus is not mentioned elsewhere. What do you think their belief could have meant?

8. Note the writer's references to himself in 1:17; 2:9; 3:10-11; 4:6-8. Where is he? Is he alone? Does he think that his life is nearly over? What is his attitude?

34. Titus

1. Where is Titus, according to 1:5? What is he to do?

2. What personal qualities are sought in elders, according to 1:5-9? Note that a "bishop" is apparently included in this group. How would you explain this? Cf. Topic 32, questions 4, 7.

3. Note the advice for various groups in the church, in 2:1-15. Why do you think the writer places so much emphasis on character and proper conduct? Cf. 1:16.

4. How should Christians behave, according to 3:1-7? What Christian beliefs does the writer express in this passage?

5. If good deeds are not the basis of salvation (3:5), why do you think the writer puts so much emphasis on doing good deeds (2:14; 3:8, 14)?

35. Jude

1. In his introduction, vss. 3-4, the writer suggests that he had planned to write a longer treatise on the nature of salvation. Now, however, he has decided to send a brief, urgent letter to warn against certain persons who have gained admission to the church. These persons were evidently anti-nomians, who held that ethical conduct was not important because justification rested on faith, rather than works. Do other New Testament writings deal with this issue? Cf. Topic 18, question 10; Topic 21, question 14; Topic 29, question 7.

2. What is the meaning of "the faith" in vs. 3?

3. What point does the writer want to emphasize by the various examples that he cites in vss. 5-9?

4. What kinds of wrongs do the antinomians commit, according to vss. 10-19?

5. How should Christians act when faced with the

problem of antinomianism, according to vss. 20-23?

36. II Peter

1. What Christian virtues does the writer mention in
   1:3-11? Why?

2. What event in Jesus' life does the writer refer to
   in 1:16-18? Cf. Mk. 9:2-8. How does this reference
   help to establish his own authority against the
   false prophets and teachers (2:1)?

3. Compare II Pet. 2:1-18 with Jude 4-16. Do you
   think one passage is based on the other? Is it
   more likely that a short writing (Jude) would be
   expanded to a longer one (II Peter), or vice versa?
   Can you think of other examples in the New Testament
   in which one writing is based on another?

4. Explain the meaning of the writer's analysis of
   antinomianism, in 2:19.

5. What problem does the writer discuss in 3:1-10?
   Does his discussion indicate that he wrote early or
   late in the New Testament period? How does he deal
   with this problem?

6. Note that in 3:11-14, the writer tries to rekindle
   a strong eschatological hope in his readers. Why
   does he do this?

7. Note that the writer includes the letters of Paul
   in the "scriptures" (3:15-16). What does this
   suggest about the date of II Peter? What does the
   writer say about these letters? In what way might
   the antinomians have used Paul's letters for their
   own purposes?